MISADVENTURES

Born in East London to working-class parents as the Second World War was drawing to a close, Sylvia Smith ducked out of a career in hairdressing at the last minute to begin a life of office work. She slowly and completely accidentally worked her way up to the position of private secretary. She is unmarried with no children. A driving licence and a school swimming certificate are her only qualifications, although she is also quite good at dress-making. Misadventures *is her first book.*

MISADVENTURES

BY

SYLVIA SMITH

CANONGATE

First published in 2001
by Canongate Books Ltd, 14 High Street,
Edinburgh EH1 1TE

10 9 8 7 6 5 4 3 2

British Library Cataloguing-in-Publication Data
A catalogue record for this book is available on
request from the British Library

ISBN 1 84195 095 5

Typeset by Palimpsest Book Production Limited,
Polmont, Stirlingshire
Printed by WS Bookwell, Finland

I dedicate this book to my parents, who had the good sense to start a family half way through the Second World War.

Every story in this book is true. It was either something I had experienced or heard about.

My Father

My father was born on 17th March, 1906 in Walthamstow, London, and named Reginald John Smith. He was forty years old when I came along. I was his second child. My brother, Brian, was born the previous year but died of convulsions when he was three days old. As my mother had difficulty coming to terms with his death the doctor told my father to start another baby immediately. I am now fifty and my father is a grand old man looking forward to his ninetieth birthday. He is extremely fit and active, looking ten years younger than his age.

My father worked as a skilled wire worker until his retirement. He made fireguards and cable grips by hand but today the same job is done by machinery. He also worked a seven-day week for many years of my childhood to support my mother and me. Despite this we were quite poor, sharing a house with another family until I was twelve.

We lived in the downstairs two rooms with a separate kitchen, and used the communal bathroom upstairs. Once I had settled down to school life my mother found herself a job in a factory and we eventually moved into a rented house on a three-year lease. It was an older-style property without a bathroom. Every Saturday my father would heat up the boiler and lay a copper bath on the kitchen floor, and we would take turns to bathe. Shortly before the lease expired the landlord decided to sell his many properties and offered the house to my father at a very low price. Both my parents were working so his proposal was accepted. My father also took advantage of a government scheme to modernise such homes and had a bathroom installed at half the usual cost. A few years later my grandfather died, leaving my father a large sum of money, which he used to pay off the mortgage and buy a brand new Morris 1100 car. My parents named her 'Nellybelle' and would drive to the coast every Sunday in the summer with my father sitting on a cushion at the steering wheel as he was too short to see through the windscreen without it.

He finally retired from full-time work and found himself a part-time job cleaning cars in a local garage. Unfortunately as he grew old he became very absent-minded and would sometimes go to work wearing one brown shoe and one black. On one occasion he wore two ties around his neck.

* * *

My father had a habit of smoking in the car. Whilst driving the short distance to work one morning he threw his lighted cigarette butt out the window but unbeknown to him the wind blew it back in again. Some minutes later he saw smoke coming up from underneath him and looked down to see his cushion was on fire. He stopped immediately, threw the cushion onto the pavement and jumped up and down on it until he had put the flames out, in full view of a very interested group of people standing at a nearby bus stop.

He eventually gave up his part-time job as it became too much for him and he sold his second and last car because he could no longer afford to run it.

All his life my father had been an honest man but as the old-age pension was hardly enough for him to live on he tried to do everything as cheaply as possible. He needed a new jacket but found he couldn't afford a brand new one so he shopped in the second-hand clothing store a bus ride away. Once he had selected his garment he looked for an article less costly. On finding a satisfactory figure and making sure the assistant wasn't looking he swapped the price tags, pinning the lower one on the jacket he wanted.

As my mother contracted arthritis my father would do the weekly shopping and any errands. These excursions were sometimes hazardous.

Whilst standing at the top of the stairs on a hopper bus he lost his balance as the bus swerved and he fell down, landing in a heap by the doors. The other passengers very gently picked him up.

On another occasion he bought a four-wheeled shopping trolley because it was something to lean on but on the way to the supermarket he tripped over the wheels, banged his head on a brick wall, fell on to the pavement (knocking his spectacles off) and found he was bleeding from a small wound over his right eyebrow. A kindly young couple saw his plight and drove him home, placing his empty trolley in the boot of their car.

His last accident was in the snow as he approached the High Street. He slipped on the ice and badly cut his hand. At the same time an ambulance arrived to take an elderly lady to hospital. She had suffered a far worse fall but the policeman on the scene said to my father, 'You might as well get in too.' So he went to hospital and had his wound dressed but he didn't telephone my mother. On his return several hours later, minus the shopping again, she was very relieved to see him.

Whilst temporarily living at home I went into my parents' front room to see the one o'clock news on their large, colour TV set. The newscaster basically said, 'The Town & Country Building

Society has merged with another building society. There is absolutely no need for concern from its depositors, this is simply a merger.' My father jumped out of his seat and said, 'I've got five hundred pounds in that place! I'm going up there now to get my money back!' He dashed up the stairs to his bedroom, put his outdoor clothing on, picked up his deposit book and precisely four minutes after the broadcast he charged out of the house saying to my mother, 'I hope there isn't a queue.' An hour and a half later he returned. I asked him, 'Was there a queue?' 'No,' he replied, 'there wasn't anyone up there.' I asked, 'Did you get your money?' He replied, 'Yes. They gave me two hundred pounds cash and a cheque for three hundred pounds.' I thought to myself, 'For God's sake don't tell him cheques can bounce.'

A past boyfriend said of my father, 'I feel sorry for him living alone with two women.'

One morning in early March my mother was selecting clothing for a dark wash in her automatic washing machine. She said to my father, 'Reg. Take those trousers off. They're dirty and they're going in the wash. Go and put another pair on.' My father went upstairs and changed his trousers, giving the offending pair to my mother. In the afternoon I decided to wash my jumpers and I had a look at my father to see how clean his one was. It looked very grubby so I said to him, 'Dad. You can take that jumper off and give it to me because I'm washing mine out and your one is filthy.' He replied, 'I'll take it off tomorrow.' I said, 'No you won't! You can take it off now and go and get a clean one.' He did as he was told.

My Mother

My mother was born on 14th December, 1912, and named Lilian Violet Parsons. She was thirty-two when she gave birth to me. She is now eighty-two. She suffers mildly from arthritis and copes well with severe tinnitus. Despite these obstacles she is quite happy and outgoing.

My mother bought me expensive toys when I was a child. I can remember beautiful dolls, a costly pram and tricycle, all of which were far nicer than anything my friends were given. In later years I discovered this annoyed my father, who had been trying to save at the time.

Whenever my parents rowed my father would refer to one episode in their marriage that had annoyed him. In 1944 my mother had been evacuated to Newcastle to escape the London blitz as she was pregnant with me, leaving my father on his own. She saw the most beautiful baby carriage and didn't hesitate to buy it. Towards the end of her pregnancy my father journeyed to bring her safely home and was furious to find he had to collect such a large item. They returned by train, storing the carriage in the guard's van until they reached London. Then my father had to negotiate the Underground with its steep escalators, and a long bus ride home.

I was ten years old and my mother decided to have my fine hair permed. As soon as my hair was washed it went frizzy and stayed that way until the perm grew out several months later. She then chose to have my hair curled again, with the same result. After this second disaster to my great relief she thought it a better idea that I should only have a good cut.

I was eight years old and my mother returned to working full-time. After school I would have my tea with the family living across the road. When I was aged twelve we moved to a rented house and I became 'a latch-key kid', letting myself into the empty house to wait for my mother's return.

My mother was always very family-minded. I can remember frequent trips together to see her two sisters living in Barkingside and the occasional weekend visiting another sister in Gillingham, Kent.

One of my aunts told me of an experience my mother had at the age of eighteen. She was staying with a married sister and answered a knock at the street door. For the first time in her life she saw a black man. She screamed and slammed the door shut. My aunt had to apologise to the man, who was simply a travelling salesman, selling brushes and dusters.

Both my parents were great bingo fans. Every Friday night for several years they would play in a local hall. They were quite lucky and came home with some large amounts of money. One evening my mother won the jackpot. The manager called her onto the stage to give her the prize money. He said, 'If you can tell me who is the current President of the United States I will give you an extra fifty pounds.' My mother was very flustered and self-conscious at facing an audience and her mind went blank. She blurted out the first name she could think of and gave 'Truman' as her answer. The manager said, 'I'm sorry, but the correct answer is Lyndon B. Johnson.'

THE FAMILY TREE

MY FATHER'S SIDE OF THE FAMILY

Both sets of my father's grandparents tasted wealth. His paternal grandfather owned an inn, which provided a good living for many years, until he became an alcoholic. He eventually lost the business through his drunkenness and became bankrupt.

My father's maternal grandfather was a ladies' hairdresser. He owned a salon and had a horse-drawn carriage to take him to the houses of rich clients. He too was quite successful but there was a fire in the salon and it burnt to the ground. As the property was not insured he also became bankrupt.

My father was one of nine children, but three of them died in infancy from childhood illnesses.

My grandmother told my mother her doctor used to criticise her husband for giving her too many children. The doctor told him, 'You are not giving your wife time to recover before you start another pregnancy.' This didn't deter my grandfather, who continued getting his wife pregnant. My grandmother also said she would jump down the entire staircase in her house in the early stages of pregnancy in the hope of losing her unborn child.

My Mother's side of the Family

My mother's grandparents were a mixture of nationalities. Her maternal grandmother was a Jewess married to an Irishman. Her paternal grandmother was a Dutch woman married to an Englishman, providing the family with an English surname. Neither set of her grandparents had money.

My mother was one of eight children, but my grandmother experienced several miscarriages.

My grandfather was a seaman, leaving his wife to cope alone with the upbringing of their children during his lengthy absences. He died when my mother was thirteen, with a brother and sister younger than herself. My grandmother collected a large sum of insurance money upon his death and placed a deposit on a family-sized house in Barkingside. Her two eldest married daughters moved in with their husbands, helping her to pay the mortgage. Unfortunately my aunts eventually vacated their mother's home for rented properties, which meant my grandmother was unable to pay the mortgage with herself and three children to support. She lost the house. In later years it would have been a good investment for all the family.

CHILDHOOD

My fondest memory of childhood is when my mother and I used to visit her two sisters in Barkingside on a hot summer's day. Both aunts lived in separate farm bungalows on the edge of a huge cornfield.

I can remember getting off the train at Fairlop Station and walking the ten-minute journey along Forest Road to my aunts' homes. My mother and I would pass the farm cottages where my Uncle Jim used to live, then the piggery with the pigs grunting away behind the long hedgerow of blackberry bushes. The crickets would be singing in the grass and only the occasional car would pass us.

Once at the bungalows one of my aunts would supply a glass of orange juice and I would wander into the back gardens and look across the golden carpet of the cornfield.

Sadly my aunts are now dead. Their homes have been sold to outsiders and are lost to the family forever.

Childhood Pets

Throughout my childhood my parents supplied me with a variety of pets. First of all they bought me two-dozen goldfish and put them in the tub of an old boiler we kept in our back garden. Unfortunately it didn't have any type of window so my fish could only see the sky and spent their time swimming in the dark. I fed them daily and in the summer months all was well. During the winter, ice formed in a thick layer over the water. My father knocked a hole through it enabling me to put food in, but after a few days of swimming in freezing water I found all my fish dead, floating underneath the ice. This did not deter my parents. Instead they bought me four goldfish in a small bowl and placed it in our lounge. Once again I fed my fish daily, but sadly they grew tired of their confined living quarters which forced them to swim continuously around in circles and they would jump out of the bowl, landing on the lino. When I saw them do this I would quickly pick them up and return them, but unfortunately one by one they tried to escape whilst I was at school and unable to 'rescue' them.

After the deaths of my fish my parents bought me a tortoise and housed him in our garden shed. I fed him a variety of salad and would allow him to go for walks along our pathway. As winter approached my father explained that tortoises hibernate during the cold weather. He made a nest using straw and an old shoe box and put my pet in it, piercing the lid several times so that it could breathe. He placed the box in a dark corner of our shed and told me not to touch it until the end of March when my reptile would wake up. I looked at my tortoise in the spring but he was quite obviously dead.

My parents allowed me to have a kitten from the litter produced by my friend Susan's cat. My kitten was a Tom and I called him 'Lucky'. Unfortunately my mother had little idea how to take care of a pet and she fed him Kit-e-Kat twice daily (in those days it was only the one flavour) and would only vary his diet once a week when she would boil him some fish. Lucky must have found it extremely boring eating the same food six days a week and when he reached adulthood he was quick to move in with one of our neighbours, a Mrs Needler, who lived four doors away from us. She would leave a variety of food out for Lucky to eat and Lucky found her diet much more interesting than ours. I was very upset at the loss of my cat. My mother went to see Mrs Needler and had a flaming row with her for enticing Lucky from me. Her final words to Mrs Needler were, 'Now that you have taken our cat from us you can keep him,' which was not the result I had been hoping for.

On my fourteenth birthday my father bought me two lovebirds. They were beautiful birds but they were too frightened to leave their cage to fly around our lounge so they spent their lives sitting on their perch. They were certainly male and female. Each evening at dinner time they would make love and my father, hearing a tapping sound, would look up from his newspaper, fold it, and whack the top of the cage with it, which frightened the birds and stopped them mating.

One hot summer's day my mother put the bird cage in our outhouse attached to the kitchen before she went to work, but she didn't open any windows. On my return from school I discovered both lovebirds dead, lying on their backs at the bottom of the cage, having suffocated in the intense heat created by the hot sun shining through the closed outhouse windows.

During my mid-teens I lost interest in having pets and my parents didn't buy me any more.

1950–60

My School Days

Infants and Junior School

I was five years old and had just started school. I was playing happily in the sandpit building castles when another five-year-old girl emptied a fire bucket full of water over my head. The teacher in charge took me to the Headmistress' office where I was undressed and my clothes placed over a heater to dry. I was told to sit down and I sat naked on one of the wooden chairs. There was a knock at the door and, much to my embarrassment, a seven-year-old boy walked in. He looked at me in surprise and handed the Headmistress a message. As he left the room his eyes examined me from head to toe.

I fared much better at Junior School.

During the lunch hour one of the male teachers gave me some money and told me to get him a Kit Kat from the local shop. I did as he bade me but returned with a tin of Kit-e-Kat.

He insisted I exchange the cat food for his chocolate.

One of my classmates wasn't too bright either. When asked by the geography teacher, 'How can you tell the time in the desert?' Jeanne le May's hand shot up. The teacher pointed at her and Jeanne replied, 'By the twelve o'clock hooter.' (In those days factories would blast hooters informing their workers it was time to down tools and go for lunch.)

At the age of ten I was put in the school play as the 'north wind'. I had to stand with my arms above my head, swaying occasionally, and I had two lines to say. My parents proudly attended the play. At the end of the evening I realised I had forgotten my lines and had said nothing throughout the entire performance.

Senior School

I attended a secondary modern school for girls in the days of extended point shoes, fluorescent socks, dirndl skirts with fluffy petticoats, and Teddy Boys.

At the age of thirteen I was caught smoking in the toilets in the company of several other teenage girls during the break. We were passing the one cigarette around with each of us taking it in turns to have a puff, when a teacher came in just as I was having my turn. She took me to the Headmistress' office. I was told my parents would be informed of my misdemeanour and I was asked who else was sharing the cigarette, but I gave no reply. After a ticking-off I returned to my class. When the other girls discovered I had not let them down I became a heroine for the remainder of the day. My parents did not receive any type of communication and the incident was soon forgotten, but it was also the end of our surreptitious smoking.

Window cleaners would occasionally work at the school. As they all seemed to be aged nineteen they were soon surrounded by teenage girl pupils chatting them up, much to their amusement.

I also remember two fifteen-year-old girls had fiancés and they married at sixteen after leaving school.

1952

Rinty

I was seven years old. I lived next door to Joan, aged six. She owned an Alsatian puppy called Rinty. I asked her mother if I could take him for a walk. She put him on his lead and passed him to me.

I decided to take Rinty to the Recreation Ground as he was very keen to have a run. He raced up the road, straining at the leash, pulling me along with him, forcing me to run through the streets. I managed to steer him in the right direction and we reached the 'Rec'. I used all of my strength to bring him to a halt on the grass. As he was so energetic I decided to let him off his lead and allow him to run around freely. He did just that. He ran all over the playing fields, around the tennis courts, straight past me and out through the 'Rec' gates into the street. I chased after him and was just in time to see him turn the corner. I sped up the road looking for him but he was nowhere in sight. I made my way home wondering what I was going to say to Joan's mother after losing her dog. I need not have worried. Rinty arrived home fifteen minutes ahead of me.

A few months later Joan's mother told my family not to tell Joan but Rinty had been sold to a farmer as he had become too big and boisterous to cope with. Joan was told he had run away.

1952

Miss Gee

At the age of seven, I was sent by my parents to Miss Gee, a piano teacher who lived in the next street. My father told me he thought I would go down well at parties in later years if I knew how to play the piano. Miss Gee was deaf and in her seventies.

Miss Gee used to sit beside me at the piano wearing a hearing aid and it seemed to me that the only way she knew if I was playing correctly was to watch my fingers. She still managed to teach me. My favourite piece of music was 'The Dambusters Theme'.

I didn't like the theory at all so Miss Gee used to let me get away with my lack of written homework.

During one lesson I played a piece of music badly so Miss Gee rapped my knuckles with her baton, which hurt and made me cry. After I had dried my tears she said, 'Promise me you won't tell your parents.' I promised and kept her secret safe.

1954

Trixie

Brenda moved into the street I lived in when we were both nine years old. We were friends until I moved away with my parents at the age of twelve.

One day in early summer I knocked on Brenda's street door and asked if I could take her black-and-brown mongrel, Trixie, out for a walk over the park. Brenda said I could but not to let any dogs near Trixie as she was 'on heat'.

Trixie was full of spirit as I walked her on her lead. We were soon over the park and running across the grass, with Trixie pulling the lead at full strength. As we approached the tennis courts a huge black mongrel appeared and began to pay her a lot of attention. I tried shooing him away but he would not obey me and quickly mounted Trixie. In my horror I let the lead go and a small crowd of children gathered to watch our threesome. The park keeper came across the grass to see what all the fuss was about and I suggested that if he had a bucket of cold water we could throw it over the dogs and possibly separate them. He ignored my request and silently watched the spectacle. Eventually the black mongrel dismounted and walked away from us. I picked up Trixie's lead and took her home.

I told Brenda what had happened and she told me not to tell her parents as she feared they might have Trixie destroyed.

Some weeks later Trixie gave birth to four black-and-brown puppies.

1954

Roller-Skating

I was nine years old. It was the school summer holidays and I was spending my time roller-skating up and down the street I lived in with my nine-year-old friend Brenda.

The street I lived in was very long with a hill at the top and ideal for roller-skating. Both Brenda and I were having fun skating up and down the hill and racing round the block and down the hill again. I was thoroughly enjoying myself until I turned the corner at the bottom of our road. I had skated at top speed and the pace I had set had taken me too fast around the corner. I totally lost my balance and fell. I put both hands out to save myself and landed flat out, face down on the pavement with my right hand settling in an enormous runny mound of dog mess. When I realised where my right hand had landed, all pain left me in my disgust.

I lifted my hand out of the excreta and wiped it on some tufts of grass growing along the kerb.

Despite being only nine years old I had the sense to skate home to my parents' flat and wash and scrub my hands with disinfectant in the big butler sink in my mother's kitchen, disinfecting the sink afterwards.

1955

The School-teacher in the Forest

I was ten years old and attending junior school. The headmaster thought it a good idea for the class to see the local wildlife and arrangements were made for us to be transported one afternoon each week to a school room inside the forest.

The room was full of stuffed animals and birds in jars, and various dried fruits. The male teacher would take us deep into the forest showing us how to tell the ages of trees, how to identify each tree by its leaves, and pointing out the lairs of otters and stoats.

On one of our excursions the teacher stopped at a clearing and suggested we all have a rest. He called me to him and told me to lay down on the grass beside him, which I did. He held me in his arms, squeezed me tightly and stroked my hair. He did no more than that but I didn't report the incident to my parents or to any other school-teacher.

1958

My First Kiss

I can't remember his name or what he looked like but I can remember going to the coffee bar after school with my fifteen-year-old friend Maureen. He and his friend sat down at our table and 'chatted us up' and a date was arranged for a foursome a few evenings later. I was thirteen.

It was a crisp November evening on the occasion of our date. Maureen and I met the boys at the top of the local High Street.

Our happy foursome wandered aimlessly through the back streets of Walthamstow. Somehow we found ourselves in the cemetery picking our way through the gravestones in the darkness.

My beau and I left Maureen and her partner for a while and we sat down on a large tombstone outside the church. After some conversation he put his arms around me in the moonlight and he kissed me. I responded eagerly and did my best to return his passion. We embraced for a few minutes and then rejoined our friends.

We made our way to the main road and parted company without making any plans for the future.

I was quite pleased with my experience but my pleasure turned to anger when Maureen told me my boyfriend was only twelve years of age and not the older teenager I had thought.

1959

Beth

I met Beth when she joined my class at school. We were both fourteen. Her mother had died so her father had Beth and her younger brother placed with foster parents because he was not able to look after them.

Beth was blonde and very pretty and a very knowing fourteen-year-old. We became friends and went out together after school hours and at weekends with both of us wearing the latest fashions, which were dirndl skirts with puffy petticoats underneath, or pencil-slim skirts.

Beth and I had no trouble in meeting young men. I would talk to them and go out with them occasionally but I would not do more than kiss them. If Beth liked her young man she would have sex with him. She had only just moved to the area and she told me she had already had several affairs with boys whilst she had been living at home with her parents.

One weekend Beth took me to see her married sister Mandy. Mandy was heavily pregnant with her third child. Beth told me she had been, and still was, having sex with her brother-in-law whenever he could see her, but of course Mandy knew nothing about this.

1959

Brian

Brian was a twenty-one-year-old Teddy Boy who rode a Lambretta. I was a fourteen-year-old schoolgirl and we met in a coffee bar. I went out with him once.

I used to go to the coffee bar with my friends of an evening and Brian was usually there with several other Teddy Boys. I accepted his offer of a date and a few nights later we met outside a greengrocer's shop around the corner from my home as my father didn't allow me to have boyfriends.

I climbed onto the back of Brian's Lambretta and he drove me to his family home. He showed me into the lounge and told me to take a seat while he selected some LPs for the record player. I settled down in an armchair and he left the room to make some coffee.

The house was small with just a lounge, kitchen and hallway downstairs and, I guessed, two-bedroomed with a bathroom upstairs. There was no sign of his parents so I decided they had gone out for the evening, leaving just the two of us indoors.

Brian returned with two coffees and sat down in the remaining armchair.

For a while we sipped our coffees and chatted and listened to the music. My cup empty, I remained in my chair innocently talking to Brian about my life in general. At his request I sat on his lap and kissed him. His kisses soon developed into gropes and I spent the rest of the evening resisting his advances. He already knew my age.

My parents did not allow me to be out later than 10.30 p.m. so at ten fifteen Brian drove me home and stopped at the bottom of my street. I got off his Lambretta and gave him a quick peck on the cheek and crossed the road as he drove away.

I did not see my father in the darkness. He was standing on the other corner of the street and had witnessed our 'goodnight'. He was furious with me and slapped my face and I was not allowed out for a fortnight.

1959

Jennifer

Jennifer was a very attractive redhead who I sat next to at school. We were both fourteen and we went out together a couple of times.

One day after classes Jennifer said to me, 'Why don't we go up the Assembly Hall Saturday? There's always a dance on and there's stacks of fellers there.' I agreed. On the special day we donned our best dresses, stilletto heels, and make-up, and back-combed our hair into the latest bouffant hairstyles.

Jennifer was right about the dance. The hall was full of men under the age of twenty-five and we spent the evening jiving to a rock group playing on the stage.

We met two young men who we discovered were friends. Jennifer particularly liked 'her one'. 'My one' was a nice enough young man of twenty and I jived with him. We were able to speak to each other when the music slowed down and we did a type of shuffle. I innocently began talking about my life at school and how my father would not allow me to stay out late until finally he asked me, 'How old are you?' I replied, 'Fourteen.' He asked, 'And how old is your friend?' 'She's fourteen too,' I replied. He continued dancing with me until the music stopped then he said, 'Thank you' and returned me to my seat. He rejoined his friend who was standing beside Jennifer and told him, 'These two girls are only fourteen.' Jennifer's young man made his excuses and both men walked away from her. She came over to me. She was very annoyed and said, 'Why did you tell him our ages? I told my feller I was eighteen and we were talking about going out with one another. Now it's all over.'

1960

Carol D

Carol and I were childhood friends, living in the same street until I was aged twelve and my family moved to another part of Walthamstow. We kept in touch until we were sixteen and became involved with long-term boyfriends. We were both fifteen at the time of this incident.

My first job on leaving school at the age of fifteen was as a trainee hairdresser. I worked in a salon for a three-month trial period but I turned down the offer of an apprenticeship as I found the work to be uninteresting.

One Sunday afternoon I walked through the back streets of Walthamstow to Carol's family home. We spent our time drinking tea and catching up on gossip until she asked me to trim her blonde, shoulder-length hair. I agreed and Carol supplied me with a pair of scissors.

Unfortunately I had only watched hair being cut and had not actually tried it myself. Carol was my first attempt. She said she would like one inch taken off the bottom so, scissors in hand, I snipped away at the right side and then did the same with the left. I looked at the finished result and saw the left side was shorter than the right. I trimmed the right side again, only to discover I had cut too much off and it was now shorter than the left. Carol gasped and put her hand over her mouth as she saw me slowly ruin her hair. I just could not get the hang of it and merrily clipped Carol's beautiful locks, one inch out each time, until I reached her ears. Trying to make a good job of my disaster I finally decided to layer what was now a short bob.

Carol's finished hairdo was a complete mess and she said to me, 'If it wasn't so funny I could cry.'

She found it necessary to pay the hairdresser a visit and she was asked, 'Whoever cut your hair for you?'

1961

Hazel

Hazel was thirty years old and married. She worked as an audio secretary in the busy Typing Department of an engineering company. I was sixteen and the office junior in the same department.

I would collect the typed letters from the secretaries' trays and deliver them to the relevant executives for signature. As I reached Hazel's desk I would sometimes stop to chat. She would tell me of her single days and of her various boyfriends. One story I particularly remember involved her father's sense of humour. She told me that at the end of one of her dates she took longer than usual saying 'goodnight' to a boyfriend in the porch of her parents' house. After some twenty minutes had passed she heard the street door opening behind her. She turned round and instinctively grasped the hot water bottle her father thrust at her. He closed the door, leaving Hazel and her beau to take the hint.

1961

Mick

Mick was eighteen. I was sixteen. We met whilst working for the same engineering company in north London. I was a junior in the Typing Department, he was a clerk in the Buying Department, the next office to mine. We dated for two and a half years.

Our office hours were 9 a.m. to 5.30 p.m. At nine twenty-five each day I would collect correspondence for typing from the various departments. I would frequently see Mick hurrying along the corridor, having overslept again. He had numerous warnings about his lateness but this did not affect his conduct. His boss eventually tired of him and Mick was sacked. He found himself a job in a hardware store. This time he had learnt his lesson and arrived on time each morning.

Mick bought a series of old cars that he and his brother Ron would repair and make roadworthy. None of them were very reliable but they were all Mick could afford. When they became too expensive to run he would sell them for scrap and buy another one.

I can remember a trip to Clacton on Sea in an old Ford. I held a piece of silver paper in the battery on the floor to keep it charging. If I had not done so we would have slowed to a halt. I did not see much of the countryside as we travelled to and from the coast.

I nearly had an accident in one of Mick's cars. He took a sharp left which forced me to lean on the passenger door and it flew open. He grabbed me just in time to prevent me falling onto the road.

Mick bought a large blue Bedford van and placed a seat beside his for me to sit on, but he didn't nail it to the ground. All was well until he made an emergency stop at the traffic lights. My seat fell backwards and I sped along the floor until I hit the doors. Once again Mick reached out to me. He seized my right ankle and pulled me to my original position.

After one evening out we were returning home in another old car when it ground to a stop in Forest Road, Walthamstow. We were lucky to find several men to push us down the steep hill by the Fire Station, whilst Mick worked the accelerator and clutch. We coasted down the hill but the car refused to start. We pushed it into the kerb and Mick walked me the short journey home. The following day his father set out to repair the vehicle and discovered we had run out of petrol.

Mick was the lead guitarist in the Dave Clarke Five shortly before they became famous. He was not happy with the band. He told me, 'I'm altering the music sheets to fit all the instruments but I don't get any more money than the others. I've seen Dave about it but he won't pay me. So I've said I'll be leaving as soon as he finds a replacement.'

A few months later The Dave Clarke Five made the hit record, 'Glad all Over'. Mick was very envious.

1961

Linda W

Linda and I worked as office juniors for the same engineering company. We were both sixteen and began a friendship that still exists today. I knew her before she met Dave, her husband. They had three children and emigrated to Australia in 1979. After twenty-six years of marriage and three grandchildren they divorced. They now have new partners.

Every evening Linda and I would travel home together. We usually caught the same bus and sat upstairs. Linda would pay the minimum fare but this did not cover her full journey. The conductress finally realised. When Linda remained seated at the last stop covered by her ticket the conductress climbed the stairs and said to her, 'You've only paid for half the distance you want to travel, haven't you?' Linda blushed furiously but remained silent. The conductress rang the bell and said, 'You can get off at the next stop.'

* * *

Linda and I went on a shopping trip down Walthamstow High Street in search of underwear. We entered a draper's and an assistant came forward to serve us. Linda said in a very loud voice, 'I want a pair of drawers.'

I paid Linda and her young family a visit in the tiny tumbledown house they were living in. Dave was finishing his dinner at the dining table in the small lounge whilst the three children played on the carpet. Linda decided she needed to be on the other side of the room, but her two-year-old daughter was blocking her path. She lifted her leg over the child. As she was wearing Dr Scholl's sandals the body of the shoe hung down giving Pamela a hearty whack on the head. Pamela cried. Linda and I laughed. Dave said, 'Try to be a mother, Linda!'

Linda decided she would like to learn to knit. She was very ambitious, choosing a sweater for Dave as her first garment. She completed the front and back and put the two pieces together to measure them. She found one was three inches longer than the other. Linda thought this was easily rectified. She picked up the scissors and began to chop off the surplus length. She was quick to realise she should not have done that.

1961

Carol C

Carol and I worked together in the same engineering company. We were both sixteen and employed as office juniors. We are still friends today.

Early in December Carol asked me, 'What day is Christmas Day?' I replied, 'I don't know.' The following morning she told me, 'Christmas Day is on the 25th of December.' I replied, 'I know that, but I thought you meant what day of the week.' She didn't believe me.

Carol and I shared our office with a girl called Jean. The three of us would go dancing on a Saturday night. Jean and I paid Carol's expenses because she told us, 'I can't afford to go out.' It was some weeks before she told Jean, 'I'm saving up really hard because I'd like a car, my own flat and some nice clothes.' Neither Jean nor I had any money in the bank so we stopped providing Carol with free entertainment.

* * *

Carol very kindly lived with me at my parents' house whilst they were on holiday. After an evening out we returned to my home and found we had no milk. She said, 'I'll go to the machine in the main road and get a pint.' Half an hour passed and I began to wonder if she'd had an accident. Eventually there was a knock on the street door. I opened it to see Carol holding the milk and a blond young man standing beside her. She told me his name was Mick and that they'd just met. They went out together for several weeks.

Carol told me one of her father's funny stories. She said, 'During the war my father was in the army and his unit was based in England. They had a fierce battle with the Germans flying overhead dropping bombs on them. One of our fellers took fright and jumped into a truck and drove away. My father said it was funny because the feller had jumped into the ammunition truck and hadn't realised it.'

Carol decided to learn to drive a car. On the day of her test she left the office early. The following morning I asked her, 'How did you get on yesterday?' She replied, 'I had the most terrible examiner and he failed me. As far as I'm concerned I should have passed. I answered all his questions correctly and I didn't do anything wrong. I was just unlucky to have a test with a creep like him.'

A few weeks later Carol invited me to the home she shared with her parents, brother and sister. I discussed her driving test with her brother and I commented, 'It was just hard luck she got a lousy examiner.' He laughed and said, 'The real reason why she failed was because she had a crash half way up Tottenham High Road. She was told to take the next left but she was in the overtaking lane and the car beside her wanted to go straight ahead. She should have let him go first but she didn't. She crashed straight into him and made a dirty great hole in the door beside the examiner. Her instructor was livid when he saw the state of the car.'

Carol married at the age of nineteen and her son, Larry, was born in the first year of the marriage. He was three months old when Carol told me, 'I thought I'd give Larry a bath in the baby bath. I put it on the kitchen table and I dipped him in it, then I covered him with soap. My hands were soapy too. I picked him up to give him a rinse and he slipped straight through my fingers and went crash on the floor!'

Each Christmas I would buy Carol some type of toiletry set. She told me her mother would say, 'Well, you know what you're going to get off Sylvie this year – another bar of soap.'

1962

The Wrestler

I was seventeen and on a date with my boyfriend, Mick. He was nineteen. We went to the Finsbury Park Empire one Saturday night to watch the wrestling. It was in the days when the matches were genuine and not 'fixed' as they appear to be now. At that age I thoroughly enjoyed the agony suffered by the wrestlers.

Mick and I were sitting approximately ten rows from the ringside. The wrestling was first class.

The third bout of the evening was between two heavyweights who were fairly evenly matched. It was a close fight until one wrestler hurled the other into the air. All fourteen stone of him flew across the ring, with legs wide open, until he crashed down on to the top rope, landing on his scrotum. At that very moment his eyes met mine. I was standing up with the rest of the crowd, clapping my hands, cheering and smiling, completely delighted at his misfortune.

He made no sound as he fell off the rope onto the canvas clutching his testicles. His pain must have been tremendous but still he was silent. Eventually two Seconds carried him to the floor. They walked down the aisle to the dressing rooms backstage, each man standing either side of the wrestler, holding an arm, while he walked like a Cossack dancer, unable to stand, without making the slightest murmur.

1963

Ursula

I was eighteen. Ursula was twenty-six. We both worked for the same chemical company in London's West End as their printing department. I ran the Gestetner Department. Ursula was in charge of the Photocopy Department. We shared an office called The Print Room.

Ursula was dark-haired and very attractive. She had come to London from Liverpool with her fiancé Eric as his job as an engineer required him to work there for six months. They were living together in a furnished flat in Streatham. Ursula told me this was against her parents' wishes.

We were both newcomers to the company. Ursula arrived two weeks after I had been employed. We hit it off from the start and as our jobs did not require much concentration we spent most of the day in conversation.

Every evening we would leave the office together, walking to Baker Street tube station, and would say 'goodnight' in the entrance. Ursula would take the right tunnel down to the trains and I would take the left. Our nightly ritual continued for some three months until one Thursday evening. I had boarded my train and was standing by the doors as they were closing, idly watching the crowds filling the platform. To my amazement I saw Ursula walking through the passageway. She saw me too. We burst into laughter as we realised we both wanted the same train. The doors closed and I jokingly waved to her as we left the station. It was several minutes before I stopped laughing, much to the puzzlement of the other passengers.

1963

The Beautiful Waitress in the Italian Restaurant

I was eighteen and working in the City as a shorthand secretary to a firm of chartered accountants. Most lunchtimes I would eat in an Italian restaurant three minutes' walk away.

The beautiful waitress who served me was Italian and aged about twenty-two. She had long dark hair, huge brown eyes, a smooth olive skin and a very slim and attractive figure. She was engaged to marry another Italian and the marriage took place some months later. She soon became pregnant with her first child.

Every lunchtime I spent in the Italian restaurant I would see the beautiful waitress tucking into plates of pasta or eating large dishes of peaches and cream. As well as her expanding pregnancy she began to get very fat and once her child was born she didn't diet to lose her excess weight. Her beauty was destroyed by layers of fat around her cheeks and jaw, under her chin and all over her body. Gone was the beautiful face and slim attractive figure.

I continued eating in the Italian restaurant and the beautiful waitress became a fat Italian mamma.

1963

GLORIA

Gloria and I both worked as secretaries in a chartered accountants in the City of London. I was eighteen. She was twenty.

Gloria and I shared an office and we would chat to each other as we worked. She told me, 'At my last job the accommodation wasn't up to very much and we had single toilets in the passageways. One day one of the male clerks went to the loo. The door was unlocked so he opened it and saw one of the Directors sitting on the toilet with his underpants and trousers around his ankles. He said he was sorry and closed the door but he told half the office and the story spread like wildfire. It must have been very embarrassing for the Director but we all had a good laugh.'

Women Travelling on Their Own in the Sixties

I was in my twenties.

The tube trains in the rush hours were packed solid with passengers travelling to and from their workplaces. I would rarely find a seat and no man would offer me his so I would usually spend my journey 'strap hanging'. During these years men stealthily assaulting women in the crowded aisles was commonplace. If I was unfortunate enough to board a full train and had to stand in the area by the doors I could expect some man to misbehave himself, unnoticed by the people around me, as we swayed to the rythmn of the train.

I can remember two incidents that happened to me. On the first occasion it was winter. I was squashed against the doors with the man to my right staring at me. I avoided his gaze and concentrated on looking through the windows. As the train drew into my stop I looked down to step over the gap between the doors and the platform and saw my admirer gently playing his fingers over my crotch. I realised he must have been doing this for some time because he smiled at me and followed as I left the train, giving me the impression that he thought I'd enjoyed his attentions and wanted more. I ignored him totally and lost myself amongst the crowds. I had felt nothing through my thick coat.

Another time I was 'strap hanging' in the aisles and a man of Eastern appearance was thrusting himself against me, again without anyone else noticing. I lost my temper and elbowed him in the stomach as hard as I could. I looked round at him in time to see his face contort and he made a whooshing noise as my action forced him to breathe out. He did not trouble me further.

Travelling at night had its hazards.

At weekends my last overhead train left the main line station in the City at 12.50 a.m. I did not experience any problems from the other passengers as I travelled the twenty-minute journey to my home town but as I walked through the side streets there was always a man behind tracking me, presumably having fun, because no one ever caught up with me or spoke to me. If I walked faster so did he. If I slowed down he did too. This game of 'cat and mouse' would continue until I reached the main road near to my parents' house. Then I would run the short distance to them.

Travelling on the last bus from Ilford was again problem-free but walking the fifteen-minute journey from the depot was unpleasant. I can remember a scruffy man aged about forty-five following me. Once again, if I walked faster so did he, if I slowed down he did and if I looked in a shop window in the hope that he would pass me, he would stop and do the same until I moved on. This behaviour continued along the main road but as I walked through the dark back streets to my parents' home he began to catch up with me. I became very angry and silently thought, 'Oh, so you think you've got me, do you! Well let's see what you are going to do!' I spun round to face my assailant and marched straight up to him. He dashed past me, turning right into one of the streets ahead of me. As he had worried me I thought it wise to walk the long way round where there was better lighting and continue along another main road. This road had a hill, a valley and another hill. I reached the top of the first hill and I could see my would-be attacker walking up the far hill. I realised he must have run half the way there. Yet again I reached home safely.

1965

A Family Health Problem

I was twenty. My father was sixty. We both had the same ailment.

To my disappointment I found I had an embarrassing complaint that needed medical attention so I made an appointment to see my doctor.

I sat down in his chair and said, 'I appear to have some growths immediately outside my backside and they itch.' He asked 'Could you be more specific and describe them?' I replied, 'They're very large bubbles of skin that look like pink grapes.' He replied, 'You quite obviously have piles. I'll write out a prescription for some cream and I want you to squeeze it into the opening of your back passage.'

A few weeks went by uneventfully until my father found he had the same problem. On his return from the surgery I asked him, 'What did the doctor say?' He replied, 'He said I had piles but he didn't ask me to describe them as he did with you. He said, "Drop your trousers, bend over and part your cheeks." So I did.' He laughed and asked, 'Supposing he'd said that to you? What would you have done?' I replied, 'I'd have kept my lumps to myself and come back home immediately.'

1965

Jean Pierre

Jean Pierre was a Swiss student who chose to live in London to improve his English. We met at a dance and dated for three months. He was twenty-three. I was twenty.

I found Jean Pierre to be very courteous and considerate. I would see him three evenings a week and each night he would take me somewhere expensive in London's West End.

On one of our dates he told me he had taken a girl in Switzerland to the cinema and she had fallen asleep half way through the film. He was so annoyed he didn't disturb her at the end of the picture but quietly vacated his seat, leaving her to wake up alone in an empty theatre.

1966

My Twenty-first Birthday

I was living at home with my parents in a small two-bedroomed house in Walthamstow, London. As my twenty-first birthday approached, I asked my father if I could have a party in the house. He told me to hire a hall as he thought his furniture might be damaged. I was very disappointed and considered what other celebration I could have, as I had always found parties in halls to be cold and impersonal, and I did not have the money to hire a suite in a good hotel.

Fortunately I had a man-friend called Frank, who was aged thirty-one. I would see him occasionally and he would call me 'Princess'. When he heard I would not be celebrating my birthday, he asked if he could take me to dinner. I was delighted.

On my special day, I opened all my birthday cards and presents. Frank had sent me an imitation silver key and had bought me a bottle of designer perfume. He knocked on the street door at 8.30 p.m. and drove me in his green Mini to an expensive hotel in Epping, just outside London. I wore a black, low-cut cocktail dress with my freshly set hair piled in curls on top of my head. Frank looked very smart in a grey suit and blue shirt with a navy-blue tie.

A waiter showed us to the table Frank had reserved and gave Frank the wine list. He ordered a glass of champagne each. We both chose a three-course meal from the menu. The waiter asked Frank what wine we would have. He clearly did not know and accepted the waiter's suggestion.

Frank was excellent company and I had a lovely evening. The food was first-class and I enjoyed the soft, piped music in the restaurant. If it had not been for Frank I would have been at a loss as to how to spend my birthday. His kindness made it a very special day.

Frank married someone else a few years later.

1967

Pierre

I met Pierre at a dance in the Café de Paris near Leicester Square. I was twenty-two and he was a very attractive Frenchman aged twenty-six.

Pierre came to the table I was sharing with a girlfriend and asked me to dance.

He led me onto the floor and pulled me tightly to him, placing his hands on my rear. I didn't like this at all and said so. He altered his hold immediately and we danced in a normal manner. The band eventually stopped playing and he asked me if I would like a drink. I accepted and we rejoined my friend at our table.

Pierre and I spent the remainder of the evening talking and dancing. Finally he asked me for my telephone number and said, 'I will call you Monday at eight thirty.' As he was on holiday and didn't have a car I went home by tube with my girlfriend. She'd had several dance partners but had not found herself a boyfriend.

I really liked Pierre and looked forward to seeing him again.

On the Monday evening I sat by my telephone and at eight thirty precisely it rang. I was thrilled and picked up the receiver but to my dismay the ringing continued. Despite frantically pressing all the various buttons and speaking down the mouthpiece I was unable to answer my phone. It rang a further thirty times and then stopped. My caller had obviously thought no one was in. I decided that was Pierre. If it was he never contacted me again.

1967

Patrick

Patrick was twenty-seven. I was twenty-two. He worked as a sales rep. We dated for three months.

Patrick lived in Dagenham. As I lived in Walthamstow and owned a car, I would drive to Ilford Station to meet him half way on each one of our dates. He would travel by bus. He would then direct me to a different pub somewhere in Essex. At the end of the evening I would drive him home.

After leaving a country pub one night Patrick said, 'Take the next left.' I did so immediately. We drove through two large iron gates, down a short drive, around a circular flowerbed belonging to a large house, up the drive again and out through the iron gates and back onto the road. We both laughed. Patrick said, 'I meant on the main road. The people in that house must have thought they had visitors coming.'

1967

Kathy

Kathy and I shared an office whilst working as secretaries to four partners in a firm of chartered accountants in the City of London, before word processors had been invented. We were both in our early twenties.

Kathy and I had busy jobs and our only opportunities for having a chat were during our tea breaks or when sewing sets of accounts together. The accounts were sewn into folders with a satin ribbon threaded through the left-hand side of the front cover and were a lengthy task not requiring much concentration.

During one of our conversations Kathy told me of a secretary she had worked with in her previous job. She said, 'She was knee-deep in work and was typing hell for leather on a manual typewriter. Halfway through the day she came unstuck. When she pulled the carriage return lever at the end of a sentence, the roller shot out the typewriter and went straight through the window into the street, and we were on the second floor! She had to take the lift down to the main entrance and pick the roller up from the pavement.'

One lunchtime Kathy and I had sandwiches at our desks. I had also bought myself a yoghurt as my dessert. I was very tidy minded and decided to suck my spoon clean. I put it right side up into my mouth, gave it a hearty suck and attempted to pull it out again. To my horror it wedged itself between my upper teeth. I groaned and Kathy looked up to see my open mouth with the spoon hanging from it. I sat at my desk wondering how I was going to free it whilst Kathy giggled. As it wouldn't move forward I tried to push it further back into my mouth and to my great relief it released itself.

1967

The Lady in the Rain

I was aged twenty-two.

It was absolutely pelting down with rain as I walked home from work down Forest Road, Walthamstow. I noticed a middle-aged woman on the opposite side of the street wearing a mackintosh and rain hat, making her way along the uneven narrow pavement. There was a deep puddle in the kerb beside her. A car drove through it at speed creating a high wall of water that drenched her from head to foot. I expected to see some reaction from her but there was none. She continued along the highway completely soaked but as though nothing untoward had happened to her.

1967

Anne

Anne and I worked for the same bank in the City. She was a copy typist in the banking hall and I was secretary to the Managing Director. She was aged twenty. I was twenty-two.

We had a big collection for Anne when she announced she was leaving the bank and emigrating to Australia. As she had a club foot she was not eligible for the Australian ten-pound assisted fare scheme for immigrants, so she chose to fly there, meeting the airline bill out of her own pocket. We all wished her well and told her to write and let us know how she was faring.

Three months later a mutual colleague saw her in the street and asked her, 'What are you doing here? You're supposed to be in Australia!' Anne replied, 'I did emigrate to Australia. I went to Sydney and found myself a small flat but I flew home again the following week because a woman got murdered in one of the flats below mine and I was too frightened to stay on all by myself. Now that I'm home I've had time to think and I'm going back again when I've saved up enough money, but not to Sydney next time. I think perhaps somewhere not quite so big will be safer.'

1968

JACKIE

I was twenty-three and secretary to the Managing Director of a bank in the City. Jackie was a twenty-year-old clerk working in the banking hall of the same bank.

Jackie was very popular and had made close friends with most of her colleagues. She was engaged to be married and had planned a honeymoon in Spain. On the Friday before her wedding day various members of staff sewed 'L' plates onto the back of her coat and ribbons onto the front. She was presented with an expensive glass clock as a wedding present from everyone in the bank.

Jackie didn't return to the office two weeks later as expected. Her new husband phoned her supervisor to say she was ill. Twelve days passed and he phoned again with the terrible news that Jackie had died.

We were told that Jackie had been taken ill on honeymoon. A doctor had been called but he could find nothing wrong with her. On their return to the UK Jackie's condition did not improve. She was examined twice in hospital but still no one could find any explanation why she was unwell. A few days after her last hospital visit she died. The coroner's verdict was that death had been caused by the contraceptive pill she had recently started taking.

Her friends in the office were in tears and those on the pill were saying, 'That could have happened to us.'

1968

ALAN

Alan was a blond twenty-five-year-old Australian journalist working in London. I was aged twenty-three and we met at a dance. He was the illegitimate son of an English woman and was adopted soon after his birth. His step-parents emigrated to Australia when he was three years old. I had four dates with him.

Alan lived in Kensington, which was known as 'Kangaroo Valley' because of the great number of Australians living there. On each of our four dates he insisted on collecting me from my home in Walthamstow and escorting me to the West End of London for dinner. At the end of the evening he saw me to my street door and returned to his digs at a very late hour. I calculated that he spent three hours travelling every time he saw me.

During the course of one of our evenings out Alan discussed sex and life in general. His final comment on the subject was, 'When I was five years old my teachers used to smack me because I masturbated during playtime at school.' He paused and looked at me and said, 'You don't understand what I'm talking about do you?' I replied, 'Yes I do.' He grimaced and blushed furiously. When he had recovered himself he changed the conversation completely.

1968

DAVID

David was a twenty-year-old police constable living in a police section house in London. He was an only child and was born in Cheltenham. Gloucestershire, where his parents still lived. I was twenty-three years old when I met him and we went out together for several months.

One wintry Saturday evening David was on duty in Knightsbridge with several other policemen. One of the officers came up to him with a civilian by his side and said to David, 'This feller has been caught stealing, guard him until I come back to you.' David took the man's arm and led him into a shop doorway. Whilst standing with his prisoner David noticed a drunk staggering up the road. He turned to the thief and said, 'Wait here while I pick up this drunk.' David walked up to the drunk, arrested him, and returned to the shop doorway, to find his prisoner was no longer there. He looked around him and saw the man running at top speed down Knightsbridge. David immediately blew his whistle and, after the intervention of his colleagues, the thief was once more in police custody.

One weekend in early summer I drove to Cheltenham with David in my black Hillman Imp car, having been invited to stay for the weekend with his family. I found his parents to be very warm and friendly and his mother had quite obviously spring-cleaned the house for our arrival. Unfortunately this spotless image was shattered over dinner as I watched her stub out her finished cigarette in her used dessert plate.

During my stay I met one of David's friends, who was a local policeman. He asked David, 'What are your chances for promotion up in London?'

1968

ERIC

He was thirty-three. I was twenty-three. We met at a dance in the winter. He lived in Ruislip. Regardless of the snow and ice he would drive across London to take me out three times a week. We dated for two months.

Eric told me he had recently been engaged to a girl and they had bought a house together in Ruislip, living as man and wife. As his fiancée got on so well with his mother, it was decided she should move in with them permanently, giving up the tenancy on her small council flat.

Unfortunately for Eric his fiancée's feelings changed towards him and she ended their relationship, returning to London to start her life afresh.

Eric said to me, 'Now I'm buying a house and I'm stuck with my mother living in it.'

1969

PAT

Pat was twenty-six. She lived at the bottom of my street with her eighteen-year-old brother and fifteen-year-old sister. Their parents were dead and Pat was legally her younger sister's guardian. I was twenty-four.

Pat and I walked to the railway station together every day on our journey to work. One wintry morning I made my way through the ice and snow to her street door. I asked her, 'Can I hang on to you? If I don't I reckon I'm going to fall over.' Pat replied, 'I think I'd better hang on to you as well.' We linked our arms together and picked our way down her pathway. Pat closed the gate behind her. She took one step forward and completely lost her footing, landing on her backside whilst still hanging onto my arm.

Pat was continually late for work and her boss had given her several warnings. He noticed her slink to her desk fifteen minutes after the correct time once more and called her into his office. He asked her, 'Why are you late again today?' Pat replied, 'It wasn't my fault. The train didn't stop at Liverpool Street.' She returned to her desk and suddenly realised that Liverpool Street was a main line station and the final stop for all trains travelling there.

Pat decided to change her job and registered with an employment agency. She was given a timed typing test. The interviewer said 'Go' and pressed the stop watch. Pat typed as fast as she could and wondered why nothing had been printed on her sheet of paper. She looked down to see she had jammed all the keys of the manual typewriter.

I went dancing with Pat and her friend Angie. Pat said to me, 'Angie gets all the fellers and I don't get any.' I examined her appearance and said, 'I think it's your hair. Why don't you have it cut?' She took my advice and made an appointment with a hairdresser one lunchtime. Pat chose a very short style to replace her long black page-boy. On her return to the office a male colleague stopped her and asked, 'What have you done to all that beautiful hair? It really suited you.'

Pat told me she walked past a family welfare clinic just as a young mother took her baby out of the pram. The woman turned around with the baby in her arms and banged the child's head against a telegraph pole. She looked at Pat and said, 'If I do that one again there won't be much point going in will there?'

1969

Bob

Bob was thirty. I was twenty-four. We met at a dance at the Empire ballroom in Leicester Square. We had one date.

Bob invited me to dinner at his flat one Thursday evening and we made arrangements that he would meet me by car at his local underground station.

He cooked an excellent medium rare steak and french fries, served with a dressed salad and a glass of claret.

After our meal we settled in his lounge with the remainder of the wine. I found him to be far too amorous. I turned down his advances and would do no more than kiss him.

At the end of the evening he drove me back to the tube and suggested I meet him there the following Thursday, but this time with a pound of sausages as he would have no time for shopping.

The next Thursday I arrived at the underground station at the appointed hour but there was no Bob. After waiting forty minutes and not knowing exactly where he lived and still there was no Bob, I went home, taking my sausages with me.

1970

John H

John was someone I met at a dance when I was twenty-five and he was approximately twenty-eight. Our relationship lasted precisely three dances.

John had a strong cockney accent and his chat up line was, 'I work for the BBC.' I looked at him in disbelief and he explained, 'Barking Borough Council.'

1970

Heracles

Heracles and I met at a dance at the Café de Paris just off Leicester Square. He was a Greek aged twenty-seven. I was twenty-five. He had a university degree in Economics and had moved to London for three years to perfect his English. He worked in a Greek shipping office in the City during the day and studied at college two evenings each week to learn the language. He shared a flat in Tottenham with another Greek and he made a lot of friends in the Greek community in London. We fell in love but we both hurt each other. He forgave me but I was unable to forgive him and he returned to Greece at the end of three years.

Heracles introduced himself to me as 'Hercules' as he found people had difficulty in pronouncing his name. I laughed and said, 'There's a TV programme called *Steptoe & Son* and Hercules is the name of their horse.' So he told me his real name. It's very easy to say.

The 'H' is silent. You then say 'error' and join it to the surname of John Cleese the actor and you have the name 'Heracles'.

Heracles' command of English was always very good and I don't remember a time when he misunderstood me, but little problems would arise. Tuesday night was the evening he chose to study and I was invited to his flat if I sat quietly beside him while he did his homework. I didn't stay silent very long but the invitation remained. He would ask me questions, one of which was, 'How do you say, "sit on the bitch"?' I replied, 'You can say, "sit on the beach" spelt B E A C H, which is the sand beside the sea, or you can say, "sit underneath a beech tree", B E E C H, but you can't say, "sit on the bitch," B I T C H, because it's a female dog.'

I taught Heracles to drive my car and he passed his test first time. This was strictly a result of my tuition as he only had two lessons before we decided I should teach him. Every Sunday we would go out for the day, frequently to Windsor, with Heracles at the wheel. On one of our weekly excursions we were travelling through central London when I suddenly doubled up in agony with fierce stomach pains. The pains did not subside and were so intense Heracles decided the best thing we could do was find a hospital and get me there as quickly as possible. He saw the 'H' sign and followed the directions, taking me straight to Casualty.

One of the nurses took charge of me. She ushered me into a cubicle and told me to take all my clothes off, put on the paper dress she passed to me and wait for a doctor to come and see me.

The doctor was absolutely beautiful. He was aged about twenty-eight, blond with blue eyes, very handsome and Australian. He asked me to lay down on the couch and he examined me over my paper dress. He pressed different parts of my stomach and asked, 'Does this hurt?' and, 'Does it hurt now?' Each time I replied, 'No.' He looked down at my legs and said, 'No wonder there's no pain, you have your legs crossed. Would you please uncross them?' which I did. He touched me again and this time it hurt.

The doctor put on a pair of transparent rubber gloves. He said, 'Now I'm going to give you the examination that Princess Anne had recently when she had an ovarian cyst. Would you open your legs please?' As I realised he was going to put his hand inside me I exclaimed, 'Oh, no! Do I really have to go through this?' He replied, 'It will only take a minute.' I resigned myself to my fate and silently allowed the doctor to do as he thought necessary. When he had finished he took a brown medicine bottle off one of the shelves and gave it to me saying, 'I want you to take two teaspoonfuls of this medicine every four hours and if the pain goes away within three days then all you have is wind. But if the pain does not go away then you have appendicitis.' He paused and said, 'You can put your clothes on now and go home.'

Back in the car with Heracles I took a huge swig of the medicine. One hour later I had no pain. As the day passed by and still I had no pain I slowly realised that I'd had wind. I said to Heracles, 'I went all the way through that terrible examination by that tasty doctor and all I have is wind. Why couldn't he just have told me to go to the loo and do my best to have a good blow?'

Heracles went home on the third Christmas and I received a letter from him in mid-January. He had worked out all the numbers for me to dial on my telephone in London and had written, 'When you are alone in your office please dial the following numbers and I will be at the other end.' I didn't do as he told me. I thought to myself, 'There's no way I'm going to misuse an office telephone by phoning Greece.' Instead I wrote him a polite and friendly letter, not mentioning the telephone.

A few weeks later I received another letter from Heracles, this time suggesting I had a holiday in Greece, staying at a hotel. He wrote, 'Then perhaps I will have the honour of showing you around.' I didn't take up his offer because I thought I should have been invited to his home, and again I wrote a polite and friendly letter but not mentioning the holiday.

I didn't expect a Christmas card from Heracles and I hadn't bought him one. When I received his card four days before Christmas I rushed to the card shop and sent him one but I must have been far too late for the last post to Greece so my card probably reached him some time in January. Heracles stopped writing to me and I guessed he must have decided I didn't want to hear from him.

I kept his photographs, letters and cards in a box in my dressing table. They stayed there untouched for twenty years before I looked through them again. I re-read the last Christmas card Heracles had sent me. He had written, 'Time is passing by, but memories remain. I remember you and every moment of the quite long time we spent together . . .' Then for the very first time I realised how much he must have loved me and I sat and cried.

1970

Heracles' Friend Chris

Chris was twenty-seven and a Greek living in furnished accommodation in Hackney. He was a friend of my Greek boyfriend, Heracles, who was also twenty-seven. I was twenty-five.

Heracles, Chris and I would go out together occasionally. One evening Chris told us of an accident he had experienced in his bedsit. He said, 'I decided to cook my dinner and I chose sausages and baked beans. I had the sausages cooking slowly under the grill and the tin of baked beans was in a saucepan of water on a low gas. I thought I had time for a shower whilst my food was cooking. When I was in the shower I heard a big explosion. I grabbed a towel and went running back to my bedsit to find the tin of baked beans had exploded. There were baked beans up the wall, baked beans on the ceiling, baked beans up the curtains. Everywhere I looked there were baked beans. It was then I realised I should have pierced the tin before I heated it in the saucepan of water.'

1975

Peter

Peter was aged thirty-six. I was thirty. We both belonged to the same social club. He was a northerner living with his sister and brother-in-law in London.

I frequently saw Peter at club events. One evening I sat beside him at the dinner table in a Greek restaurant. We were deep in conversation and he told me, 'I don't really like London. I much prefer the north but I was forced to come here. In my home town I had a girlfriend who I was potty about and she lived at home with her parents. Every night I saw her her parents would go to bed early and leave us alone downstairs. As soon as they went upstairs me and my girlfriend would have sex in their lounge. I really loved her and wanted to marry her but in the end she chucked me in. I was alright about things to start with but she found herself another boyfriend and it really did my brain in because I realised she was having sex with him in her parents' lounge as she'd had with me and I just couldn't handle it. I used to go to her house every night to see her but she'd shut the door on me and leave me on the doorstep. I'd keep banging on the door and her father used to come out and he'd give me a good talking to and then he'd shut the door on me. I'd still keep banging but they all ignored me. Then I'd phone her all hours of the night but they'd just slam the phone down. I was in a right state and I couldn't stop myself. In the end her parents called the police and they sorted me out. I still couldn't handle the fact that she was having it off with someone else but I knew if I made a fuss about it I'd have finished up in court so I came down to London.' He laughed and said, 'I couldn't give a damn about it now.'

Pauline

Pauline was a sixteen-year-old office junior in her first job from school. We both worked for the same refrigeration company. She soon found a boyfriend in Clive, one of the young men working in the Stores Department. I was thirty years old and shorthand secretary to the Company Secretary.

Pauline started dating Clive. As he was her first boyfriend she very sensibly went to see her doctor and arrangements were made for her to go on the Pill.

After taking the Pill for three months Pauline realised something was wrong and returned to her doctor convinced she was pregnant. The doctor asked her why she thought this and soon discovered her mistake. 'My dear,' he said, 'when you take this particular Pill you are not supposed to take it every day of the month. You are supposed to take it for twenty-one days and then stop taking it for seven days and during these seven days you should have a period.

The reason you have not had a period for three months is because you have taken the Pill every day. I am quite confident you are not pregnant.'

1975

Josie

Josie was twenty-five. I was thirty. We met at a charity club and became friends. Every Friday evening we would go to a local disco. At one of these evenings Josie met Ken. He owned his own house two streets away from my parents' home and was a divorcee with two young children, who lived with their mother. He let furnished rooms in his home and had two male lodgers. The following is what happened on Josie and Ken's first date.

Josie and Ken liked each other from the moment they met. On their first date Ken collected Josie from her family home and drove her to a country pub. At the end of the evening he invited her to his house for a coffee.

They sat in Ken's lounge sipping coffee and talking and listening to the music playing on the stereo. Eventually Josie sat on Ken's lap and they kissed and cuddled. After some time had passed Josie broke free from Ken's embrace and looked at her watch, to see it was early morning. She said, 'I'll have to go, Ken, as it's very late and my mother might worry about me.' She stood up and her eyes focused on a large red bloodstain on the left leg of Ken's white trousers. Josie was terribly distressed and blushed furiously. Ken looked down at his trousers. Josie said, 'I'm sorry, Ken. I must have cut myself or something.' Ken replied, 'I don't think so. Don't forget I've been married and I know what it's all about. I know what you've got.' 'Well, I'm really sorry,' stuttered Josie. 'This has never happened to me before.'

Ken said, 'I'd better take these trousers off and put them in the washing machine and find myself another pair to wear.' He left the room saying, 'I won't be a minute.'

Unfortunately, Josie didn't have any more tampons with her, thinking she was sufficiently protected. She turned her skirt round, only to see it was very messy at the back. Ken returned wearing blue denims and said, 'I'd better put some newspaper on your seat in the car just in case.'

Ken drove Josie home while Josie sat on several sheets of newspaper. He stopped the car outside her house. She said to him, 'I'm really sorry about this evening, Ken.' Ken smiled, kissed her on the cheek, and said, 'Don't worry about it. I'll phone you.'

Josie alighted from the car and to her acute embarrassment she found the sheets of newspaper had stuck to the back of her skirt. She eased them off and took them into the house, waving goodbye to Ken as she walked up the path.

Despite this eventful first date, Josie and Ken dated for three months.

After their relationship had ended Josie said to me, 'Do you know, I never saw Ken's white trousers ever again.'

1977

The Man at the Funfair

I was thirty-two.

It was a beautiful summer's day so my friend Linda and I decided to go to the funfair. It was very crowded and noisy with the different music and sounds of the fair. Linda and I played on the various stalls and slowly walked around the fairground looking at all the amusements. We stood near the swinging chairs and watched the people get into them. Once they were full the music started up and they gradually swung out higher and wider. Underneath them stood a middle-aged man with his suit jacket over his arm. He looked up at the chairs now swinging directly over his head. At the same time somebody above him vomited. The vomit landed on the man's face and trickled down his shirt-front and on to the jacket he was holding. Linda and I grimaced as we watched him wipe himself with his handkerchief.

1977

Hilary

Hilary and I met through a social club. She was twenty-six. I was thirty-two. We went out together until her marriage to Mike and the births of her two children, a boy called Elliott and, two years later, a girl called Francesca. We are still friends today but only see each other occasionally.

In her single days Hilary owned a car that the garages appeared to be unable to repair. She would drive for twenty minutes and then the engine would cut out and she would slowly come to a halt. Hilary tried several garages but still this fault was not rectified so she decided to sell the vehicle privately for the large sum of eight hundred pounds without telling the prospective owner of this defect. She provided a test run and luckily this went without a hitch. The buyer was delighted with his purchase and paid Hilary the requested amount. The negotiations completed, Hilary watched from her front gate, heaving a sigh of relief as her car disappeared in the distance. She heard nothing further of her sale.

Hilary and Mike decided that Elliott should have a first birthday party. They invited close friends and family, and several mothers and babies Hilary had met at the Welfare Clinic, accompanied by the fathers.

Halfway through the party Elliott's grandmother picked him up from the carpet where he had been playing with his little friends, sat him on her knee, and spoon-fed him a strawberry yoghurt. Elliott very contentedly sat on her lap eating the yoghurt. As he finished one spoonful he opened his mouth wide waiting for the next one. All was well until he had emptied the tub. His open expectant mouth turned into a pucker and he sat on his grandmother's knee sobbing his heart out.

On one of my rare visits to see Hilary she told me, 'I took Elliott and Francesca swimming when Francesca was four years old and she shit herself in the pool. I don't think anyone noticed because most of it was in her swimsuit but I got her out of the water as quickly as possible and took her to the loo.'

John S

John was forty, I was thirty-two. We both belonged to the same large social club. He frequently organised weekend trips in Europe for other club members. I met him when I joined his party on a trip to Belgium. He was tall, dark and handsome. He loved women, and they were attracted to him. I heard rumours that on every trip he organised he always found a lady to share his bed.

John was a very good tour organiser although he charged everyone a few pounds extra so that he had a free holiday. Our trip that weekend was to Brussels and we were a party of twelve.

On our last night we dined in an Indonesian restaurant and the food was excellent. I noticed John continually glancing around the room. He finished his dinner and left our table to join two unknown foreign girls seated in another part of the restaurant. At the end of the evening he returned to pay his bill and left with the girls, taking them to our hotel. He persuaded his room-mate to squeeze into another room with two other men from our party and John spent the night having sex with both women. On our return to London the following morning he slept the entire journey on the coach, only waking when we reached the ferry.

Ten years passed before I saw John again. This time he was organising a club disco. He was still a very attractive man but unfortunately he was almost bald and this did not suit him. His baldness obviously embarrassed him as he had grown long locks of hair on the left side of his head and had brushed them over his crown in an attempt to disguise his lack of hair.

I felt very sorry for him because he was very much a ladies' man and his bald head showed the beginning of his decline.

1977

Lorraine

Lorraine was my ex-boyfriend's sister. She emigrated to Canada at the age of nineteen and lived with her Canadian father's relations. We met when she was twenty-six and on holiday in London for two weeks, staying in her parents' house. In Canada she ran a second-hand clothing store with one of her Canadian uncles. I was thirty-two.

Lorraine began life in Canada living with her uncle, his wife and their two sons. Her relations showed her the sights and one Sunday her cousins took her to a lake for a picnic and swim.

They laid their picnic on the grass at the water's edge and soon all three of them went into the lake. Lorraine didn't know how to swim so she decided she would just have a paddle, but unfortunately she slowly waded out of her depth. By this time her cousins had returned to the shore and their picnic. As Lorraine was unable to rejoin them she frantically shouted and waved at them whilst she jumped up and down desperately trying to keep her head above water. Her cousins smiled and waved back at her until they suddenly realised her predicament and swam out to rescue her.

Thankful to be on dry land again, Lorraine sat on the grass getting her breath back. Her relief at being saved from near-drowning was marred when one of her cousins said to her, 'Your bikini top is around your waist.'

Lorraine attended a family gathering at her Uncle Haddie's house in the country. After a couple of hours had passed she paid a visit to the bathroom and discovered a huge stool floating in the toilet. She used the toilet brush and flushed the system several times to clear the stool but to no avail. Her visit to the bathroom was immediately followed by her Uncle Haddie and Lorraine told me, 'I didn't feel comfortable all afternoon.'

1977

Nasrin

Nasrin was Indian and the divorced mother of two teenage girls. We met through a social club. She was thirty-eight. I was thirty-two.

Nasrin and I sat beside each other at a pub event. We were soon in conversation and she told me of an unpleasant episode in her life.

Nasrin had a bad marriage for many years and eventually divorced her husband. The court decided she should have the family home and custody of her daughters. Her ex-husband was very bitter because he had lost everything; his wife, his house, to a certain extent his children, and his money, as he was forced to live in a furnished room because he still had to support his family.

One weekday when the family home was empty he let himself in with his key. He entered the lounge and removed two photographs from their frames and then went upstairs into the double bedroom he used to share with Nasrin. He opened the wardrobe door and picked out all Nasrin's photograph albums and loose photographs which she kept in a box at the bottom of the wardrobe. He sat down on the bed and tore each photograph into fragments and cut through all the negatives with scissors. His task completed, he left the house.

Nasrin came home and saw the remains of her photographs on her bedroom carpet. She told me, 'If my husband had wanted to hurt me then he found the perfect way of doing it. He destroyed all my photographs and negatives and now I have no photographs whatsoever to show my past life. I used to have waist length hair but I have no photograph to remind me, and I have no photographs of me as a child, or of my daughters as babies, or of my wedding, or of my relations. He completely ruined every single photograph I possessed.'

1978

BETTY

Betty and I belonged to the same large social club. We met when we joined a club party travelling to Yorkshire for a weekend break. She was forty. I was thirty-three. She had recently returned to the UK from the US to attend her mother's funeral. She had emigrated to the US six years earlier with a girlfriend. They had made their home together until the friend married, leaving Betty to live alone in their apartment. Although Betty considered life in the UK to be dull in comparison, she did not return to the States as she had found it increasingly violent and felt she was too old to start again.

On Betty's return to the UK she moved in with her father, sharing his council house in Dagenham. She told me, 'My father had six children and apart from me they've all married and had families and he's done everything for them. He's helped all his children out whenever they've needed it and he's made Wendy houses, cots and toys for all the grandchildren and apart from my sister Anne who does his shopping once a week, none of them phone him up to see how he is or to invite him over for the weekend. They don't bother with him at all. At Christmas he goes to Anne for the day and she gives him a present but all he gets from the others is a Christmas card and that's about their only contact.'

Betty put her name down for a council flat. She said to me, 'There's no way I'm living with my father until he's too old to look after himself and I'll be the one who has to nurse him.'

A few weeks later Betty was offered accommodation in Barking and promptly left her father's home.

1979

Glyn

Glyn was a forty-year-old Jamaican who was self-employed as a car mechanic. He lived in the next street to me and occasionally worked for me. He was married with two young sons. I was thirty-four.

Glyn continually asked me to go out with him but I always refused. He would frequently complain about his marriage, telling me that his wife only allowed him sex once a month, how frustrated he was and that he was looking for a discreet girlfriend but had been unable to find one.

I moved away from the area and heard no more of him until I met one of the neighbours who told me that Glyn and his wife had divorced after he had poured a can of petrol over her and had tried to ignite it. Their house had been sold and his wife had custody of the children but Glyn did not go to prison.

1979

Sam

Sam was a fifty-five-year-old sales rep. We were both employees of the same clothing company. I was thirty-four and private secretary to the Managing Director.

As I entered the showroom I heard Sam talking to the Sales Director. He was explaining why he'd been late for an appointment with a client the previous evening. He said, 'I broke down in my car last night.' I interrupted and asked, 'Didn't you have a hankie?' which brought some humour to the situation.

1979

Malcolm

Malcolm was thirty-eight. I was thirty-four. We met at a social club event and dated for two months but there was no romance between us. We became 'good friends'.

On our third evening out together Malcolm took me to the cinema to see the latest film. He bought our tickets and said to me, 'I must go to the loo. I won't be a minute.' I waited in the foyer and looked at my watch as the time went by. Twenty minutes passed before he came out of the gents' toilet. He was not at all embarrassed and simply said, 'I'm sorry,' as he led me in to see the film, which fortunately had not started.

On the way home from the cinema Malcolm and I were discussing our various romances. I told him I had dated over one hundred men before the age of twenty-five and that they had all been platonic relationships. Malcolm could not believe this at all and said, 'You should have had sex with them all!' I replied, 'You must be joking! If I'd had sex with all of that lot I'd have a face full of spots by now. I prefer to have serious relationships.' Malcolm said, 'The next time you go out with a man just relax, lay back and let him do it.'

1979

Brian G

Brian, Phyllis and I were members of the same social club. He was a divorcee aged forty-two and had been engaged to and living with Phyllis for some time. She was ten years younger than him. I was thirty-four.

Brian and I attended a ramble event in Epping Forest one Sunday morning in summer. I noticed he arrived in a bright, shiny new car and without Phyllis.

The ramble was very well attended, making a group of twelve people. After struggling through the undergrowth and muddy footpaths we eventually stopped at a country pub to quench our thirst, choosing to sit on the wooden benches outside. I sought out Brian and settled beside him. I said to him, 'That was a nice car you were driving.' He replied, 'It was. I only bought it about a month ago but some nut smashed into it, so the novelty has worn off.' I said, 'Oh, that was bad luck.' He continued, 'That car is the first car I've ever bought brand new. I literally spent weeks looking through catalogues to find myself exactly what I wanted. I was really pleased with it. Then this idiot crashes in to me at the traffic lights. I was stationary and waiting for the lights to change and he comes along not looking where he was going and drives straight into the back of me. He made a huge dent in the boot. Alright, the garage did a good repair job but that car now seems to me to be second-hand and I've lost all pride in it.' I sympathised and said, 'Well, it's still a beautiful car.'

I changed the subject and asked, 'No Phyllis today?' He looked down at his drink and replied, 'No, she's busy.' I asked, 'Is she cooking your dinner?' He replied, 'That's right.'

We spoke to the other club members and I overheard Brian saying, 'I'm living with my father at the moment.'

1979

Club Row Sunday Market

Mr and Mrs Porter were the parents of my ex-boyfriend Neil, who died after a long illness at the age of thirty-two. We became friendly and I called them 'Mr and Mrs P'.

One Sunday morning I joined them on their weekly excursion to Club Row market, travelling there and back in Mr P's car.

Mr P was a lousy driver, not being able to see too clearly, but apart from going through a set of red traffic lights and successfully avoiding a collision with the three cars travelling towards us, our journey was uneventful. We reached our destination and he parked in one of the side streets. Mrs P and I left him in the car and set off on our shopping trip.

As we neared the market we saw a traffic warden writing out a ticket for a vehicle illegally parked. A man from the group ahead of us called out to him 'Shouldn't you be in church?'

1980

Mr and Mrs P

Mr P was Canadian. In later years he was crippled with arthritis – wearing leg irons and using crutches to help him walk. He had been a soldier based in London during the last war, where he met Mrs P. They began married life in Canada but Mrs P could not tolerate the isolation of the countryside and returned home with one-year-old Neil. Her husband quickly followed her and they settled in London, having a daughter, Lorraine, some years later. Lorraine emigrated to Canada at the age of nineteen. I was twenty-seven when I first met Neil and his family.

Shortly after Neil's death I fell out with my parents and moved into Mr and Mrs P's home as a paying lodger, an arrangement that suited all three of us.

Mrs P worked part-time in a factory and spent the remainder of her life in her kitchen watching a black and white TV set. At this time Mr P was crippled and sat in an armchair in the lounge during the day watching a coloured television and eating the meals his wife served him on a tray. At night he slept in the second reception room downstairs as the upstairs bedrooms were too difficult for him to reach.

I found Mrs P to be a very unpleasant woman. After living in her home for a few months we ceased to be the good friends we had been and would simply acknowledge one another. Every Friday I gave her my rent I expected her to give me notice to leave but that didn't happen.

Mr P and I had tremendous fun. I shared his lounge most evenings and we would make jokes and have two pence bets on whether a certain celebrity had died or who they had married. He usually lost his money. The day before I left for a skiing holiday he said, 'I hate to tell you this Sylvia, but it's been on the news that there are terrible avalanches in Austria and some people are stranded out there for possibly another week until they can clear the snow.' I realised he was joking and laughed, but he continued, 'If I were you Sylvia I'd contact your travel agent.'

It was a Tuesday morning shortly before Christmas. I was about to leave for the office when there was a knock at the street door. As Mrs P was still asleep and Mr P had difficulty walking, I opened it to see a middle-aged man holding out a cap. He asked, 'Would you like to donate?' Thinking he was some type of charity worker I replied, 'No thank you,' and closed the door. I hastened around, picking up my handbag and car keys, and left the house, saying 'Goodbye' to Mr P. As soon as I returned in the evening he called out to me, 'Sylvia, that feller knocking on the door this morning was one of the dustmen and he was asking you to give them some money for their Christmas box. As you turned him away, when he emptied the dustbin in the cart instead of putting it down gently in the front garden he threw it all the way up the path until it hit the street door.'

All three of us became aware we had a problem. The electric light bulb in the lounge wore out and it was decided I was our only hope, despite the fact that I had no experience of looking after a house and was unable to do the most simple of tasks. Mrs P brought the ladders in – she was far too fat to climb them and Mr P couldn't. I clambered up them whilst they held on to me as tightly as possible. Unfortunately I don't like heights. The ladders were old and very rickety and the higher I ascended the more they wobbled. I managed to take the bulb out of its socket as the ladders swayed but I couldn't fit the new one in. After several failed attempts we realised we would have to find another solution. As the days passed by all the light bulbs in the house slowly burnt out. Luckily, Mrs P had a great variety of bedside lamps and she placed one in every room.

Our next hurdle was the washing line in the back garden. The wooden pole shattered and the line fell on to the grass. Neither Mrs P nor I knew how to repair it.

The three of us had a meeting and it was decided we should wait until we had a visitor.

Eventually Mrs P's sister and her husband called. As soon as her brother-in-law stepped into the house Mrs P persuaded him to replace all the light bulbs and repair the washing line.

We occasionally had a dinner guest. He was a young Indian Mrs P had befriended in the factory where she worked. At our request he would wander around the house carrying out minor repairs.

My relationship with Mrs P went from bad to worse and came to a head one Friday evening. I was frying sausages in the kitchen when she came in from work. She yelled at me, 'You always rush home so you can get to the cooker before me and you always sit watching the TV in the lounge when Cliff goes to bed so I can't get in there. Get out of my kitchen.' I argued, 'No, I'm cooking my dinner and I don't rush home to get here before you and as far as the front room is concerned I don't see why you don't go in there.' This upset Mrs P further. She screamed, 'Get out of my kitchen and get out of my house this instant!'

She took two steps forward and lightly punched my shoulders. As I took this to be an invitation to have a fight and I didn't relish rolling in the mud with her in the back garden, I vacated the kitchen and went upstairs to pack. As I passed the lounge Mr P said, 'I'm sorry about this, Sylvia. If it was up to me you could live here forever.' I packed my things and put them into my car parked outside, then I returned to the kitchen. Mrs P shouted, 'And don't send your father round here either.' I picked up my frying pan with my uncooked sausages in it, placed it on the passenger seat in my car, and drove home to my parents as I had nowhere else to go at such short notice.

Despite leaving his house, I telephoned Mr P at regular intervals until he died a few years later.

Michelle

Michelle was twenty-six. I was thirty-five. I had a two-week booking as a temporary secretary with her employers. I worked in the office she shared with two girls who were both in their twenties.

Michelle and the other girls made me welcome. We were soon in conversation and I settled down quite quickly.

Michelle talked as she worked throughout the day and appeared to be very relaxed and at ease. I was surprised when she told me her live-in boyfriend had found himself another girlfriend and they were separating. I asked, 'Surely you must be very upset?' She replied, 'Yes, I am but there's no point moaning about it.' She continued, 'We bought a house together seven years ago and were planning to marry when we wanted children. I thought we loved each other and he liked to go out with his friends occasionally. It didn't occur to me he was with another woman. Then last week he announced he'd found somebody else and wanted to sell the house and set up home with her. It was the most terrible shock. Ever since then I get myself drunk every night and I usually have a few drinks before I come to work and some more in my lunch hour. Right at this moment I can just about see what I'm typing, but I can't crack up. I've got to get through this and drinking helps me.'

At the end of the week nothing had altered for Michelle, who was still hiding her unhappiness with alcohol and idle chatter.

I took my time sheet into the agency on the Friday evening. My supervisor said, 'You can't go back there next week Sylvia because you are in your thirties and the girls you're working with are all in their twenties. Their Personnel think it would be nicer if they had a younger temp.'

1981

The Indian Shopkeeper

He was short and middle-aged. I was thirty-six.

I saw a beautiful green handbag in the window of an east London leatherware shop, but without its price tag. I entered the shop and asked the Indian shopkeeper how much it cost. He reached for the bag and passed it to me, saying, 'This is an excellent handbag in a very soft leather that I imported from France and I want seventy-five pounds for it.' It was much more than I had expected and I told him so. He showed me various cheaper bags but I didn't like any and left the shop.

I walked along the High Road and the Indian shopkeeper caught up with me. He fell into step beside me and we strode along the main road together. He asked, 'Can I take you for a coffee?' I replied, 'No thank you.' Undaunted he asked, 'Can I take you for a drink?' Again I replied, 'No thank you.' He then asked, 'Would you like to be my wife?' I was very surprised but once again I replied, 'No thank you.' He returned to his shop as I continued on my way.

1983

Aunt Milly

My aunt Milly was a prim and proper old lady of seventy-four, despite having been married twice and the mother of two adult sons. My mother was seventy. I was thirty-eight. The three of us had a night out together.

All three of us decided to have an evening out and we chose to go to the cinema. As neither my mother nor my aunt had much idea of what film to see the selection was left to me. I picked a Monty Python film thinking it would make us all laugh. It certainly made my mother and me laugh but not my aunt, who sat in her seat in quiet disgust with a stony expression on her face all the way through the film.

One particular tract of the film I guessed was a little too much for my aunt. Two men appeared on the screen and climbed into a cloth suit of a cow and hobbled around a field which, unfortunately for the man in the rear end of the cow, had a live bull in it. The bull didn't realise the cow was not real and galloped across the field and had sex with it. Immediately the bull had finished, the cloth cow made its escape and staggered out of the field. The man in the rear end stepped out of the suit and, after the violent thumping he had received from the bull, he was unable to walk properly. The lower half of his body appeared to be twisted and he winced as he walked with a pronounced limp. My mother and I thought the entire scene extremely funny and laughed our heads off. I turned to see my aunt's reaction. She was sitting motionless in her seat, her eyes glued to the screen without even a flicker of a smile.

After the film had ended we left the cinema and I drove all three of us home. My mother and I were still laughing about the man in the cloth suit but my aunt sat quietly in the car without making any comment.

That was the last time I took aunt Milly to the cinema.

1983

Ghalib

Ghalib was an Iraqi who had lived in London for twenty years. We met at badminton classes and became friends. He was forty-three. I was thirty-eight.

Ghalib decided to emigrate to England from Iraq and he chose London as his home town. Unfortunately on his arrival in the UK he did not speak any English. He enrolled immediately in English lessons. He told me it was one year before he was fairly fluent and able to stop asking people to repeat themselves. He also told me of his first trip on the London Underground. He said, 'I went down the tube to go on a fairly short journey and I got totally lost. It took me four hours to find my way out again.'

Some time later Ghalib entered into a disastrous three-year marriage with an English woman. He described the relationship to me saying, 'She stepped into my life, ruined it and then stepped out again.'

Ghalib also told me of a recent relationship he'd had with an older woman. He said, 'She was fifty-six, divorced, and had a thirty-year-old son. Our sex life was usually good but one evening we were in bed having sex together when she suddenly "blew off" and I found it so off-putting I was unable to perform and that was the end of our sex that evening.'

I used to play badminton at the sports centre every Monday evening until I sold my car and the journey became too lengthy. Ghalib very nicely offered to take me in his car every week so my badminton evenings continued. He was always asking me for a date despite my continuous, 'No thank you, Ghalib, I don't want to be anything other than friends.'

One Monday evening as Ghalib was driving me to the sports centre I noticed how crestfallen he appeared and I asked him what was wrong. He said, 'I have just fallen in love with the most wonderful woman, Sylvia, but I am almost ill with worry because she has run away from me and I can't find her. I've tried phoning her lodgings but she's not there any more. I feel so bad I've been to see my doctor and he's given me tranquillisers. I just cannot bear this.' I looked at his ashen face and said, 'I'm very sorry, Ghalib, but instead of having her on your mind all the time why don't you try forgetting her?' 'I just can't,' he replied. Our evening continued but he played badminton in a very subdued fashion and he drove me home making only brief replies to my conversation.

As I was worried about him I phoned him later in the week and asked, 'How are you, Ghalib?' He replied, 'Oh, I'm feeling better now but the situation has not resolved itself. I managed to find my lady but she refuses to see me. When I finally managed to speak to her on the telephone I told her how overwhelmed I had been by my feelings for her and she said the reason why she'd run away from me was because she'd been overwhelmed as well and had been unable to cope with her feelings for me.' I asked, 'How are things now?' He replied, 'I'm afraid it's over, Sylvia. She just won't see me any more because it's all too much for her. But, oh, I remember how we hugged each other in the moonlight. It's so very sad.'

To a certain degree this put my nose out of joint as I had always thought Ghalib was mad about me. It was a slight shock to find he had amorous thoughts in another direction and I was no longer on his mind. Curious, I asked, 'How long did your relationship last, Ghalib?' 'It was only one date,' he replied.

1983

Jenny H

Jenny and I became friends when we lived in the same furnished house. I had the bedsit downstairs in the front of the house and Jenny shared the garden flat behind mine. One year later she bought a one-bedroomed flat a short walk away. We continued our friendship. She was thirty-two. I was thirty-eight.

Jenny had a long-term boyfriend called Dave who owned his own property but preferred to live with Jenny in her small apartment. She told me, 'He's a lousy lover. He smokes thirty cigarettes a day and when we have sex he has to stop halfway through and have a rest for ten minutes to get his breath back.'

Jenny told me Dave was filled with remorse when his father died. She said, 'Dave's father suffered from depression. Dave saw him talking to someone in the street about a week before he died and Dave walked straight past him, ignoring him completely. A few days after that his father went to Dave's flat but Dave wouldn't let him in and told him to go away. The following week his father hanged himself and Dave can't get over his guilt. It plays on his mind that he should have helped him and perhaps if he had then his father might still be alive today.'

1984

Ian

Ian was an eighteen-year-old bank clerk who wore Brer Rabbit fun slippers behind the counter as he served his customers. The other bank staff voted him 'the sexiest backside in the bank'. I was thirty-nine and a temporary secretary for the same bank. He had a flair for telling jokes. Here is one of them.

'There were two punk rockers strolling through Trafalgar Square. One punk rocker said to the other, "What would you do if a bird shit on your head?" The other punk rocker thought for a minute and then said, "If she did that to me I don't think I'd want to see her again."'

JANET

Janet was a married woman in her fifties and the mother of four adult children. I had a three-month booking as a temporary secretary in her office in the probation service. I was thirty-nine.

Janet was a very kindly and pleasant woman. Despite knowing me for ten days precisely she bought me a pot plant on my birthday.

One of Janet's daughters took a year out of university to teach English in China whilst improving her Chinese. As Janet and her husband hadn't seen her for several months they decided to holiday there. Janet flew, arriving many hours later, but her husband was so frightened of flying he travelled by train, arriving a few days later.

Janet said to me, 'My second daughter told me she was leaving home to share a flat with some friends and I said to her, "Good luck dear, and don't forget you will always have a room here."

Then I fell asleep in the armchair whilst she was packing. She came to say goodbye to me and I was still asleep. She woke me up and said, "When my friend June left home her mother was in tears," and I said, "Oh, I'm sorry dear." She was quite offended.'

My booking finished and my agency sent me to various other probation offices as I understood the work. Occasionally I had reason to telephone Janet and I noticed how abrupt and barely polite she was. I eventually returned to her branch but worked elsewhere in the building. I asked one of the secretaries, 'What's the matter with Janet? She's not at all like her old self. Every time I speak to her she's just about civil and she gets rid of me as quickly as possible and doesn't really want to talk to me.' Her colleague replied, 'Her marriage is finishing. She's getting divorced and she's sorting out with her husband who gets what and I don't think Janet wanted the marriage to end.'

1985

The Probation Service

I had a three-month booking as a temporary shorthand secretary in a branch of the probation service. I was aged forty.

I found working in the probation service very interesting but it also had its darker side. In this particular branch, thirty chairs were nailed to the floor in the large reception area as a past offender had smashed a chair on top of a probation officer's head, fracturing the man's skull.

I shared the office in reception with five other secretaries. Halfway along one wall there was a wide opening where we would speak to the clients as they came in. It was fitted with iron shutters to be pulled down and locked should there be a disturbance.

One afternoon all the probation officers were out attending meetings or appearing in court, leaving the six secretaries on their own with just a middle-aged clerk in his office in the long passageway adjacent to reception. A drunk stumbled in asking to see his probation officer and was politely told by a secretary that the officer was in court and no one else was free to see him but he could leave a message. This infuriated the drunk who shouted abuse at the secretary and started thumping the frame of the opening with the flat of his hands. At the same time the clerk stepped out of his office to go on an errand. The drunk turned and saw him and lurched towards him, focusing his shouting and swearing at him. This frightened the clerk who ran up the corridor desperately trying all the doors to find one unlocked, with the drunk now chasing after him. He frantically tried another door and, to his great relief, it opened. He quickly entered the office and locked himself in at top speed. The drunk, still shouting abuse, pounded his fists on the locked door in the hall while the clerk remained inside, too frightened to face him. Eventually the drunk stopped his pounding and staggered down the corridor, past reception, still shouting abuse, and out into the street. Hearing the drunk walk away and silence in the hall, the clerk unlocked the door and went about his duties. The comment from the supervising secretary was, 'He's not much of a man, is he? He leaves us secretaries to cope with an aggressive drunk while he hides himself away trembling with fear.'

* * *

Another afternoon all the probation officers attended an AIDS-awareness demonstration. Each officer was supplied with a banana and a condom and they were taught how to use a condom with the banana representing a penis. Once they had mastered this art the idea was that they would show their clients how to do so correctly, thereby reducing the risk of them catching AIDS through casual sex.

I was offered a job at that probation office but I considered the salary too low and I didn't like their set-up of a supervising secretary being in charge of the daily workload and of all the other secretaries, which would have included me.

1985

My Investments

I reached the age of forty. It was such a milestone I took a hard look at my past life. I felt I hadn't done very much with it. I had never married or lived abroad. I had led the life of a single woman, having nice clothes, nice holidays, nice cars, nice evenings out, and, despite the fact that several men had fallen in love with me, I'd had few romances. I thought to myself, 'What can I do about this? I don't want to get to sixty and find I still haven't done anything worthwhile.' I decided I would like to achieve something and I thought, 'What can I achieve?' My next thought was, 'How about I make myself rich.'

I decided to make long-term investments which I hoped would eventually make high profits. I bought one hundred shares each in five leading British companies and I slowly bought large blocks of Premium Bonds because I thought 'How else can I make a hundred thousand pounds?' Also, I saw an advertisement in a newspaper which stated that if I invested in a leading bank's investment scheme and put down at least a one hundred pound deposit and invested a minimum of twenty pounds per month over a period of nine years, my money would treble. I considered this investment to be a first-class idea so I filled in the bank's form, enclosed my deposit and sorted out a Standing Order with my bankers.

Six years passed by. During this time I made approximately sixty pounds a year in premiums from my shares. I won fifty pounds four times on my Premium Bonds and I had continued investing my twenty pounds monthly. Then the recession caught up with me. I was made redundant by a building company and I returned to temping halfway through the summer, which is usually the busiest time for temps, only to find there was no work available. Despite trying my best to find work, I was to be unemployed for the following two years.

Faced with unemployment pay of thirty-nine pounds a week to live on I decided to look at my investments to see if they were worthwhile.

I went to my bankers and spoke to one of their executives. I said, 'I have a lot of shares in various UK companies and I'd like to sell them subject to the shares being worth at least as much as I paid for them. So could you tell me the selling prices before we start filling in forms?' The executive consulted a newspaper and informed me that all my shares were currently selling at half their original value. As I couldn't afford such a loss I chose to keep them in the hope that at some time in the future they would return to the price I had paid for them.

I kept my Premium Bonds as I still considered them a good idea despite only winning a total of two hundred pounds during the six years I had owned them.

I telephoned the famous bank whose investment scheme I had joined and discovered I had not trebled my money but had actually made a loss of some twenty-six pounds. I decided not to lose any further monies and cancelled the agreement. I received a cheque for the amount I had invested minus twenty-six pounds.

It was quite obvious to me that I would have fared better if I had put all my money in the Post Office and had not attempted my 'get rich scheme'.

1985

ELAINE

Elaine was a bank clerk aged twenty-seven. I worked for the same bank as a temporary secretary with a three-month booking. She was married but had no children. I was aged forty.

Elaine and I shared the same lunch break and we would chat to each other. During one of our conversations she told me she was the youngest of five children and her mother had died whilst they were all of school age. Her father didn't think he could cope with raising a large family single-handed and working full-time to support them so he gathered his children around him and said to them, 'I don't see how I can look after each one of you and keep you at the same time. I've thought about it very carefully and I've decided you will have to go into a Home until you are teenagers.'

Elaine laughed as she told me, 'We all burst into tears and cried our eyes out until my father felt so terrible he couldn't go through with it and he said, "Alright. I've had enough. I won't put any of you in a Home but we'll have to look after each other as best we can."'

Elaine told me her father continued working and managed to cook the dinner every evening and get the shopping at the weekends, leaving the children to share the household chores, with the eldest supervising the younger ones. She said that despite this she had a very happy childhood.

1986

The Neighbours

I was aged forty-one.

A middle-aged woman and her elderly mother moved into a newly refurbished house in 'our' street. We saw beautiful furnishings being carried up the path by various deliverymen.

Both women lived together very quietly, not mixing with the neighbours. The older woman was never seen and it was rumoured that the younger woman only left the house for work in the City or to buy the weekly shopping. We did not see any visitors.

The following year the elderly woman died of natural causes. Some weeks after her funeral a neighbour told me the daughter had committed suicide by jumping off the roof of the office block where she worked, the assumption being because she could not face life alone.

1987

Brian R

Brian was a thirty-eight-year-old Director of a local company. I was his secretary, aged forty-two. His wife Sue, aged thirty-six, was a solicitor. They had a four-year-old son called Simon. I worked for Brian for one year, until I was made redundant. The company eventually closed down.

Brian and his family went on a two-week package holiday to Spain. On his return to the office I asked him if he'd enjoyed himself. He replied, 'Not really, no. The first week it rained every day and all day and the second week Simon broke his arm.'

Brian and Sue attended many official dos throughout the month. I asked him, 'Wouldn't both of you rather be at home of an evening? Surely all these functions are boring?' He replied, 'Some times they're very interesting. For example, Sue went to an official dinner last Tuesday and she told me the highlight of the night was when a fellow diner vomited all over the table.'

1987

Pat

Pat was fifty-six. I was forty-two. We were secretaries in the Directorate of a local company and were both made redundant. The company has now ceased trading.

During one shared lunch break Pat chatted about her life. She told me she had been married twice. The first marriage produced a son and then a daughter, but ended in divorce. The second marriage was childless, finishing with widowhood. She now had a live-in boyfriend.

Pat told me her mother felt very proud when her grandson was born and insisted on pushing the pram on the child's first outing. Pat said, 'We were walking up the road talking away when we heard a terrific bang. We looked round to see the pram had hit a tree. We rushed to see how the baby was and he wasn't there! We took the cover and all the blankets off and we found him right at the bottom of the pram. He must have had one hell of a shock and he was only two weeks old.'

After our redundancies I had a weekly dinner date with Pat and I met Brian, her boyfriend. He was forty-seven, divorced and the father of two adult daughters. Pat told me that Brian liked his drink. He would go to the pub after work and spend the evening downing pints of beer. He would stagger home to her and would lean on the street doorbell making it ring continuously until she answered it, despite having his own key.

Pat told me that Brian's boozing got him into trouble. He had been to court several times on drink-driving charges and on his last appearance he had been sentenced to one-month's imprisonment in Pentonville and banned from driving for two years. Released from prison, he sold his car but still continued his heavy consumption of alcohol.

Brian suggested the three of us should go to dinner as his treat and the date was set for the following Saturday. Pat booked us in to two restaurants, one Greek and the other traditional English in case we didn't like her first choice.

She picked me up by car from my home in Walthamstow and drove to a pub in Hackney to collect Brian. We entered the saloon bar and heard Brian's loud voice cracking dirty jokes with the barman and some of the customers. I saw he was having difficulty standing. Brian welcomed us and ordered a round of drinks, Pat and I choosing orange juices. After much effort we managed to drag Brian away from the bar. We returned to the car and travelled to the first restaurant with Brian sitting on the back seat telling more dirty jokes. At the end of each one he would burst into peels of laughter.

We ordered our drinks in the Greek restaurant with Brian still talking at the top of his voice. His conversation turned into noisy complaints at the poor service and fifteen-minute delay of our order. Pat decided we should leave and move on to our next reservation.

Returning to the car we walked through a small green just off the main road.

I noticed Brian was lagging behind and turned to see him relieving himself over a bush in full view of the other pedestrians and the cars that sped by. Judging by the torrent of urine coming from Brian I guessed he must have swallowed at least a dozen pints of beer.

At the second restaurant we were asked to wait in the bar until our table was free. Pat said, 'I must go to the loo and I'll get the drinks on the way back.' In Pat's absence Brian looked me over. Suddenly he reached out and squeezed my left boob and said, 'Oh, what a lovely pair of tits.' I was so surprised I made no comment.

Soon we were ushered in to our seats in the crowded restaurant. Brian was quite obviously very drunk and the other diners quickly became aware of that. By this time his speech was slurred and he was almost shouting but he did manage to choose his dinner from the menu unaided.

Despite Brian's condition things went fairly smoothly until he spotted two black couples sitting at a table on the other side of the room. He yelled, 'Niggers. I don't like niggers. You dirty bastards. Why don't you go and swing through the trees.' Pat tried to quieten him down but he still continued with his abuse of black people. The other diners forgot their small talk and laughed as they listened to him. One of the black ladies passed our table on her way to the powder room. Brian bellowed, 'Go home you black bitch. We don't want you here.' The woman ignored him completely and walked by without glancing in our direction. This state of affairs amused the other diners who sat in their chairs laughing. His racist remarks continued for the remainder of the evening and the entire restaurant became his attentive audience. Finally, Brian paid the bill and Pat suggested we leave. She helped him from his seat and eased him into his jacket. On the way out we had to negotiate twenty concrete stairs leading down to the street. Pat turned to Brian and said, 'You hang on to my arm and watch where you tread otherwise you'll have an accident.' All three of us got safely back to the car.

She drove me home, she said 'goodnight' but I have not seen or heard from Pat since that evening.

1987

Ginnie

Ginnie and I met whilst on holiday in Cornwall with other members of a large social club. She was forty-four. I was forty-two. As we got on very well we went out together on our return to London.

Ginnie phoned me at work one day and asked, 'Are you any good with problems? Because I've got one and I'm really fed up.' I replied, 'Well, tell me what it is and I'll tell you what I think.' Ginnie continued, 'I went to see my doctor because I had earache and she said I had some type of infection and she gave me some drops to put in my ears. After I went swimming my ears got worse so I went back to my doctor and she said I've got to see a specialist because I've now got white spots in my ears and she doesn't know what they are. And the last time I had to see a specialist was when I had a problem with my big toe and I had to have an operation on it. Now I've got to see a specialist again and I don't want an operation on my ear,' she moaned. I replied, 'First of all, Ginnie, you shouldn't have gone swimming if you had an ear infection, it probably made things worse. But your doctor doesn't know what those spots in your ears are so she's sending you to someone who will know and I don't think you have a problem because if it was something terrible then I would think she'd recognise it. So it's probably something quite simple.'

Ginnie went to see her specialist a couple of weeks later and phoned me at work after her visit. She said to me, 'You were right. The specialist said those white spots in my ears were just my ear drop solution drying and sticking together in clumps so there's absolutely nothing wrong with my ears now, and he said to me going swimming wasn't a very good idea but everything should be alright now.'

Ginnie told me she was walking through Wood Green on her weekly shopping trip one Saturday afternoon when a young woman came up to her and asked, 'Have you got a pound I could have?' Ginnie continued walking up the road and replied, 'Do I look as though I've just got off a banana boat? What do you mean "have I got a pound"? Have you got a pound to give me?' The woman looked at her in surprise and said, 'I don't see why you're making such a fuss about it. If I had a pound I'd give it to you.' By this time Ginnie was some distance away and yelled at the woman, 'I have to go to work for my money. What are you going to do – spend all day asking people for money? You bloody scrounger. I've seen reports on TV about how you beggars get more money than everybody else.' The woman shouted back, 'Piss off you old cow.' Ginnie, still walking further away, hollered, 'Piss off yourself, you fat slag.' They continued hurling abuse at one another until they were out of earshot.

Ginnie phoned me at the office as usual. She said, 'There's a circus up Ally Pally, do you fancy going?' As I thought this a good idea I agreed and it was left to Ginnie to make the booking.

On the day of the circus we went to the Box Office, only to find Ginnie hadn't kept the reference number, which meant the clerk had difficulty finding our tickets. It would have helped matters if Ginnie had been polite, but she was annoyed and the following fifteen minutes were spent with Ginnie and the clerk exchanging snide remarks whilst he searched his records.

Our tickets located, we entered the Big Top.

The seating consisted of scores of long wooden benches joined together lengthwise. Our seats were in the last row at the back of the tent. Mine was on the end of one bench and Ginnie's was on the other. Ginnie's bench was empty except for a woman some ten feet away with a child on her lap. As soon as the band began to play the woman bounced the child up and down in time to the beat. This action resulted in Ginnie bouncing up and down too. I thought this to be hysterically funny but Ginnie was not amused. When the music stopped she retaliated by bouncing up and down on her seat. This did not alter the woman's behaviour. Eventually I squeezed up on my seat and Ginnie sat beside me.

1987

Andrea

Andrea was twenty-six. I was forty-two. We both lived in Jenny F's house as lodgers. Jenny was forty.

Andrea amazed Jenny and me. She had a university degree in sociology but worked as a waitress. Jenny said to her, 'Why don't you write to some companies and tell them your qualifications and ask them if they have a vacancy for you?' Andrea never bothered and continued in her menial job.

Andrea was not very hygienic. After work she would have a quick wash in the bathroom, cleaning just the basics and her dusty feet, leaving a tide mark all around the basin. Each time I shampooed my hair I had to scrub the bowl before using it. She would rarely have a bath. Although Jenny supplied a first class automatic washing machine Andrea would change her bed linen and bath towels very infrequently.

Jenny said to me, 'Every time I come home I can see Andrea's dirty net curtains upstairs as I come up the path. She hasn't taken them down for months. I'm going to put them in the washing machine a couple of times.' Jenny opened Andrea's bedroom door and found the smell to be so bad she grabbed a bath towel from the airing cupboard and held it over her nose as she removed the curtains. I told her Andrea had spilt a can of lager on to the carpet but Jenny replied, 'She's just a dirty cow, Sylvia.'

Andrea and I would chat in Jenny's kitchen after work. One evening we were discussing our backgrounds. She told me, 'My father died soon after I was born and my mother died when I was four so I was brought up by my grandmother. As she's now dead too my only other relative is an aunt I haven't seen for years.' She paused and continued, 'I felt sorry for my grandmother. She was a very ambitious woman. She had tremendous drive and always wanted to get on in life. Unfortunately for her she married a man who was quite content to have an everyday job and to go up the pub for a drink as his social life. He never achieved anything at all and my grandmother had to settle for life in a council house and a humdrum working-class existence. She died alone and a very bitter woman.'

Andrea and I decided to go out one Friday and

we chose ice-skating in London's West End. We met immediately after work, dining in one of the many restaurants in the area, ending the evening in a local pub. The pub was very crowded. I noticed a group of five young men drinking at the bar. Suddenly four of them grabbed the remaining friend and tried to take his clothes off. The victim fought desperately to keep them on but he was outnumbered and was soon completely naked. His friends eventually tossed his clothes to him and he slowly dressed. The Manager of the pub went over to them and lightly said, 'Now boys, no more of that. You'll have to settle down.'

Andrea was very keen on a young man called Jonathon whom she had met at a folk club. He would telephone her occasionally but this didn't suit Andrea and she would phone him every week. As Jonathon never asked her for a date she decided to go to the folk club by herself on the night he was usually there. She was delighted to see him and sat down beside him engaging him in conversation. She invited him to sleep at her home that night and Jonathon accepted.

The following morning I woke and heard a strange cough coming from Andrea's room. I wondered who it was and if I'd been mistaken because Andrea did not have men stay overnight. I went to the toilet and saw a large pink condom floating in the water and I realised that she had a visitor.

I left for work without seeing her and looked forward to my return.

As soon as Andrea and I settled at the kitchen table with mugs of tea I asked her, 'Who was that feller you had in your room last night?' She laughed and asked, 'How did you know?' I replied, 'Well, I heard someone cough and then I saw a pink Johnnie in the loo so I guessed.' Andrea said, 'That was Jonathon.' I teasingly asked, 'Did you have a good time?' She laughed and replied, 'We did but I was a bit embarrassed about the sheets, they could have been cleaner.' She paused and smiled saying, 'I wonder if Jonathon will see more of me now?'

Jonathon did not telephone her again and was very brief when she called him. He didn't make any dates to see her and Andrea stopped going to the folk club. The relationship ended.

Jenny decided to modernise her house and make a proper home for herself instead of living downstairs in her divided lounge-cum-bedroom. She said to me, 'I'm going to take out a second mortgage to pay for everything and I want Andrea's room as my bedroom so I'm going to give her one month's notice and I won't be sorry to see her go.'

On the day Andrea moved out I waited until she had shut the street door behind her and then examined her room. It was very smelly. I saw an eiderdown draped over the lower half of her bed. Curious, I pulled it off and found two-dozen deep-red circles of blood embedded in the mattress. Jenny returned from shopping a few hours later and I told her what I'd seen. She gasped when she saw the stains and said, 'Andrea left me her new address so I could send her her deposit. There's no way she's getting a penny out of me. I'll have to get rid of this mattress and on top of that the carpet stinks so I'll have to do something about that as well.' I thought to myself, 'Did Jonathon see those circles? And how bad were the sheets he slept on?'

A few days later the builders began their work. Jenny said to one of them 'Can you take the mattress out of my upstairs front room and put it in your skip? I'm sorry about the condition of it but we had someone dirty living here.'

1987

Jenny F's Night Out

Jenny was an attractive blonde aged forty and my live-in landlady for two years. She was in the process of modernising her house so she could live more comfortably, only having one paying lodger, which was me, instead of the usual two. I was forty-two.

Jenny went to a disco one Friday evening with her friend Lynne and didn't return home until the early hours of the next day. As I had spent the week working hard and socialising I was tired and went to bed early. I woke the following morning around 9 a.m. and I was sipping my second mug of tea in the kitchen when the telephone rang. I hurried up the stairs to the communal telephone extension and found it was Jenny on the line. She said, 'I don't know what you're on but do you think you can answer the street doorbell to me in about ten minutes' time?' I replied, 'Yes, of course. What's the matter?' 'What's the matter!' she repeated, 'I'll tell you what's the matter! I came back from the disco with Lynne about three o'clock this morning and Lynne was going to come in for a quick cup of tea and I found I'd forgotten my key so I rang the street doorbell but it didn't wake you up so both Lynne and me kept ringing the bell, banging on the knocker and yelling through the letterbox and that didn't wake you up either. We were making the most tremendous racket and Lynne said to me, "How is it she can't hear us?" You just didn't wake up so I had no alternative but to go round Lynne's. When I got round Lynne's I telephoned you and I left the phone ringing and ringing and you still didn't wake up and the telephone extension is only on the other side of the wall to where your bed is. I really don't know what you're taking but I've just had to spend the night on Lynne's front room floor because I couldn't get in to my own house. I'll be round in about ten minutes. Since you are now conscious do you reckon you can let me in this time?' I replied, 'Yes, of course,' as Jenny slammed the phone down.

I replaced the receiver and I laughed and laughed. I let Jenny in when she rang the doorbell. She was still very annoyed and stormed down the hallway into the kitchen. She sat down at the long wooden table and clutched her back and groaned, 'Oh, I ache like hell.' She said, 'Lynne's floor was very uncomfortable.' She winced with pain again and I laughed out loud. She said, 'It isn't funny, Sylvia!' I said, 'When I go to sleep at night I don't usually wake up until the following morning and I sleep through thunderstorms and more or less any natural noise. I'm sorry you've had a lousy night but I can see the funny side.'

Jenny's back took several days to get better and the more Jenny winced with pain the more I laughed.

1987

LYNNE

Lynne was a forty-year-old divorcee and the mother of two teenage children. She was blonde with blue eyes, and absolutely beautiful. I met her whilst lodging in Jenny F's house as she was one of Jenny's friends. I was forty-two. Jenny was forty.

Jenny and Lynne went to Charlie Chan's nightclub to dance the night away. Jenny didn't find herself a man but Lynne did. He was a Turk called Ihan and she became his girlfriend.

Ten weeks into their relationship Lynne paid Jenny a visit. They were sitting at the dining table in Jenny's kitchen one Sunday discussing Lynne and Ihan's affair whilst I was cooking my lunch.

Lynne said to Jenny, 'I think Ihan only wants to know me for sex. Ever since we've been seeing each other I go round to his house three times a week, he never takes me out anywhere, he doesn't even buy a bottle of wine and all we do is bonk each other. He went back to Turkey a couple of weeks ago for his sister's wedding but he never bought me any type of present. I think he wants me for sex only and isn't very interested in me at all.' Jenny thought for a moment then asked, 'When did you start having sex with him?' Lynne replied, 'We had sex in the back of my car after the disco the first evening I met him and every time I've seen him since. I think I'm just being used for somebody to have sex with. What do you think?'

1988

Barbara

Barbara and I met when we shared the same furnished house. She was forty. I was forty-three. We lived together for one year and are still friends today. She had married an Italian called Adrian at the age of eighteen and lived in Italy for twenty years with her husband and three children. The marriage deteriorated and Barbara returned to the UK leaving her teenage children with their father. She spoke fluent Italian and told me she was more at home speaking Italian than she was English. At the time we lived together she shared a room with her Italian boyfriend, Luciano, who did not speak English.

Barbara and I got on very well together. We arrived home from work at the same time every evening so we would chat to each other as we cooked our dinners. She would tell me of her life in Italy.

Barbara said, 'When my youngest child, Silvia,

was two years old we were living in the mountains of Italy and my in-laws had come up to see us. It was a nice summer's evening and we were walking up the road with the children when Silvia started playing with the bars of the iron fence at the edge of the mountain. She had about six adults looking after her and the next thing I knew she fell straight through the bars and rolled about forty feet down the mountainside to the lower road. I thought she'd bloody killed herself! Adrian and me rushed down the path. I picked her up and we ran to the car and Adrian drove like crazy for about ten miles to the nearest doctor. I was shaking like a leaf but when the doctor examined Silvia he said there was nothing wrong with her at all – but he gave me a supply of tranquillisers.'

Once Barbara's young family were of school age she found herself a part-time job teaching Italian children to speak English in a classroom set in the mountains. On a winter's evening at 'home time' one of Barbara's eleven-year-old boy pupils asked her if she would like a lift on his toboggan on the twenty-minute journey down to the village. Barbara told me, 'I must have been mad but I got on to the back of his toboggan. It was pitch-black, no street lights anywhere, and we went down the mountain road in all the snow and ice and he went faster and faster until we were bombing along. When he wanted to go left he stuck out his left foot and when he wanted to go right he stuck out his right foot. I held on tight to him and tried not to panic. There was a steady stream of cars coming up the road so I said to him, "What about all this traffic?" He said, "It's alright. You can see everyone's lights before they come round the bends." I was absolutely petrified and by the time we got to the bottom of the mountain I was a nervous wreck. I staggered off his bloody toboggan and he said to me, "I bet you won't want another lift from me, Miss."'

Whilst Barbara was in Italy she had to have an operation for gallstones. She told me, 'The orderly came to collect me from the ward and put me on a trolley to take me into the operating theatre. He was running through the corridors with me when he took a corner too fast and I shot off the trolley and went crunch on the floor. He tried to get me back on it but I was too frightened and told him "No," so he jumped up and down shaking his hands saying, "Mamma mia, Mamma mia," and he had to get me a wheelchair, and that was how I went into the operating theatre.'

Barbara finally returned to London with her Italian boyfriend, Luciano. One weekend she decided to take him to Brighton. They were sitting on the crowded train chatting in Italian when

Luciano's thoughts turned to sex. He rubbed his left foot slowly up and down Barbara's right leg and this aroused Barbara. She looked at him and asked, 'Where?' Luciano replied, 'In the lavatory.' They quietly walked across the compartment to the toilet adjoining their carriage and squeezed into the tiny room. Barbara took off her jeans as Luciano dropped his trousers. In his haste he squashed her between the door and the washbasin. Barbara's foot wedged on the water release button on the floor and the small sink filled and overflowed. This did not deter them and they had sex in their cramped position. As Barbara was jammed against the door it banged every time Luciano plunged into her. Soon, passion overtook them and their rhythm echoed throughout that section of the train. With lust sated they refreshed themselves, attended to their clothing and stepped out of the closet, returning to their original seats through the still crowded compartment, speaking in Italian without a thought to the other passengers.

1988

Paula

Paula was a twenty-one-year-old black receptionist. I was a secretary to a director of the same building company. I was aged forty-three.

As I returned from lunch I passed Reception and saw Paula leafing through a large clothing catalogue. I went over to her and said, 'Hello. Can I have a look too?' She replied, 'Yes, of course. The book belongs to Irene upstairs and she's running it as an agency so if you want anything just tell her.'

Paula and I turned the pages exchanging our opinions on the various clothing until she asked, 'What colour suits you, Sylvia?' I replied, 'As I have dark hair practically every colour suits me except nigger-brown.' I suddenly realised what I'd said and in my embarrassment I quickly carried on talking about anything I could think of, while Paula nodded and smiled at me pretending she hadn't heard anything untoward. After rabbitting away about nothing for a further five minutes, I beat a hasty retreat to my office.

1988

Martina

Martina was twenty years old and from southern Ireland. Her elder brother shared a furnished house in London with three other Irishmen. As soon as a room became vacant, Martina left the family home in Ireland and moved in. We worked together as temporary secretaries in the same branch of the probation service and became friends. I was forty-three.

Martina and I went out together occasionally despite our age gap and we kept in touch after our bookings ended.

In the summer Martina returned to Ireland for a two-week holiday. As she had recently passed her driving test she persuaded a friend to allow her to borrow her car, enabling her to travel across the country visiting her scattered family.

Martina was driving at speed as she passed a shopping arcade. She looked in the window of a clothing store but turned round too late to stop at a red traffic light. She slammed the brakes on but this did not prevent her from crashing into the stationary Austin Metro ahead. Both drivers surveyed the damage. The other vehicle suffered a pushed-in boot and buckled bodywork. Steam was hissing out of the front of Martina's Ford and the bumper lay in the road. She was asked for details of her insurance but unfortunately she had not bought any.

On her return to London Martina received an invoice from the injured party's garage totalling one thousand five hundred pounds. She also had to pay five hundred pounds for the repair of her friend's car. As she had no savings she arranged a bank loan. Her brother tried to help and gave her three hundred pounds towards the bill. Martina worked overtime each evening and at weekends for the following eighteen months until she had cleared her debt.

1988

The Little Boy

Early for my appointment, I sat in Dr Birrell's surgery in Forest Road, Walthamstow, idly glancing out of the window at the busy rush-hour traffic. I heard a screech of brakes followed by a loud bang and saw a coloured boy aged about seven fly through the air and land on his back in the middle of the road. I was forty-three.

Hearing a commotion outside all the patients in the waiting room peered through the windows into the street to see a black child lying unconscious at the wheels of a car. The receptionist poked her head through her hatch then swiftly entered Dr Birrell's adjoining surgery. She telephoned for an ambulance as he hurried into the street.

Dr Birrell examined the child where he lay. Soon the little boy began to recover. Dr Birrell lifted him into his arms and carried him inside saying to his anxious patients as he passed them, 'There's no serious damage done to him.' He settled the boy on his couch and returned to the woman driver who had followed him into the surgery. He asked 'And how are you?' She replied, 'I'm perfectly alright, thank you.' He said, 'If you leave your name and address with my receptionist I see no reason why you should not go home as I'm quite sure the child has not come to any harm.'

Shortly, an ambulance arrived and the little boy was transported to hospital for the necessary check up.

The general opinion in the surgery was, 'What an ideal place to have an accident.'

An article appeared in the local newspaper the following Thursday detailing the incident. The hospital comment was, 'The child was badly shaken but had no injuries other than a few bruises and it was not necessary to detain him.'

1989

Shaunagh

Shaunagh and I became friends when we both shared the same furnished house. We lived together for eighteen months and are still friends today. Shaunagh is from Northern Ireland and a staunch supporter of the IRA. At the time we met she was twenty years old and I was forty-four. She has since returned to Derry.

Shaunagh always had a carefree attitude to life and very little upset her. Despite horrendous events happening to her she usually landed on her feet. On the rare occasion when she didn't she was quick to come to terms with the situation and once again happiness would rule her world.

Shaunagh loved to do her shopping in Sainsbury's. If the load was too heavy to carry she simply wheeled the trolley out of the store and all the way home. On one of my visits I saw two Sainsbury's shopping trolleys in her back garden.

Shaunagh loved loud music and a blaring

TV and didn't pay too much attention to the neighbours who preferred her to be quieter. She received an official letter of complaint from the local Council over the volume of noise in her home. Her reaction was to laugh, show the letter to all her friends, then dump it in the dustbin, still continuing with her boisterous lifestyle.

Our difference in accents was sometimes a problem to me, although Shaunagh understood every word I said to her. She came to my flatlet for dinner one evening and as usual we had a long chat. I told her of my black admirer across the street. 'I quite like him,' I said. 'I like the way he rides down the road on his bike with his straw hat on.' I thought Shaunagh asked me, 'Is it a posh bike?' I replied, 'Well, I don't know about that, it looks like any ordinary bike to me.' She replied, 'Well, you must know whether it's a push-bike or a motorbike.'

Shaunagh and I went to the cinema to see a Richard Gere movie as we found him to be quite attractive. Halfway through the film she was bursting to go to the loo. She delayed her visit some twenty minutes as we realised the plot was heading for a heavy sex scene and she was determined not to miss it. As the actors bared themselves Shaunagh's eyes were glued to the screen. Once they put their clothes on she dashed to the toilet at top speed.

* * *

Shaunagh shared a furnished house with a Scottish girl aged twenty-six called Sharon. They usually got on very well together, partly because Shaunagh did all the housework and turned a blind eye to the fact that Sharon didn't do any.

They did fall out one weekend when Shaunagh arrived home minus her street door key at one thirty on a Sunday morning. Sharon was with her boyfriend. Shaunagh walked to the nearest telephone box and told her of her predicament. Sharon replied, 'I can't come over to you with the key, Shaunagh, because I'm with John and we haven't got any clothes on.' Shaunagh tried to persuade her to get John to drive the ten-minute journey to their home but Sharon simply said they were too busy. This meant that Shaunagh had to spend the night in the porch of the house. She settled herself on the concrete as best she could and fell asleep in her huddled position. At 7 a.m. her next door neighbour looked out of his front room window and saw Shaunagh's legs laying down the pathway. He decided to investigate. After some discussion he said, 'I'll climb over the back fence and see if I can get into your kitchen.' He was successful and Shaunagh was at last able to get into the house. She went straight to bed and rested her aching bones.

Sharon's refusal to bring the street door key annoyed Shaunagh. She said to me, 'She was too busy having sex to come and give me the key.'

Another Saturday night ended in disaster in the small hours for Shaunagh. Once again she had forgotten her street door key and had to sleep outside. This time she didn't know Sharon's whereabouts.

Unfortunately Shaunagh had spent the previous evening drinking and eating to excess and she was desperate to go to the toilet from both front and back outlets. There were no public lavatories close to her and she felt she couldn't wake next door at three o'clock in the morning so she decided she had no alternative but to urinate and excrete on the pathway. Sharon returned home at about 4.30 a.m. and Shaunagh once again got into the house. She told Sharon how she had relieved herself, proudly pointing to the mound of excretion. Shaunagh was not embarrassed in any way and related the incident to all her friends, leaving the rain to slowly wash away her waste.

Shaunagh and Sharon went to the Irish pub in Leytonstone, a regular haunt of theirs one Saturday night. At closing time they invited various friends and acquaintances back to their home for a party. The stereo was played very loudly and the thirty guests were drinking heavily. Shaunagh was not concerned when a fight broke out in the dining room, resulting in the landlord's antique coffee table being broken and the front gate coming off its hinges as the violence spilled over into the street. Vince, the landlord, was very easygoing. When he arrived at the house later that day for the rents, he was not bothered about the table and found a screwdriver to help him put the gate back into the wall, without making too much comment.

Both Shaunagh and Sharon found Vince to be a nuisance. He was in his forties and in his second marriage, which was very turbulent. Every few weeks he and his wife would have a terrible row and Vince would move out of the matrimonial home and into the spare bedroom in Shaunagh and Sharon's home, which infuriated both girls. He would stay a few days then he would make it up with his wife and return to her. Two months later they would have another battle and he would move in with Shaunagh and Sharon again. His temporary residence at the house stopped when Shaunagh found him a third paying lodger.

Shaunagh's habit of a good drink on a Saturday night frequently landed her in trouble. She told me of her latest escapade. 'I went out with my boss and some of the staff where I work and we all finished up in the Irish pub and after that I didn't remember any more until I woke up on the Sunday morning. Straight ahead of me were the curtains and the window and I could feel somebody beside me in bed. I lay there thinking to myself, "I'm in bed with somebody and I don't recognise those curtains. Please God don't let me be in bed with my boss." I slowly turned my head to see who I was sleeping with and it was my ex-boyfriend, Booker. I woke him up and asked him what had happened and he said I was so drunk the night before I couldn't tell the minicab driver where I lived so to be on the safe side he took me back with him.'

Booker became famous overnight. He was an Irishman called Richard Berry who appeared on the TV news in the UK after he killed a pit bull terrier and assaulted its owner. He was sentenced to four years' imprisonment, spending his time in Wandsworth and Pentonville prisons before finishing his punishment in a Kent jail where he enjoyed himself feeding the pigs.

One of Shaunagh's Irish friends phoned her and asked, 'Have you got a room spare in your house for a friend of mine? He's twenty and just over from Derry and he hasn't found himself any digs yet.' Shaunagh replied, 'Someone has just moved out so we have got a vacancy and I should think my landlord would like the extra money, so send him over and we'll see.'

The formalities sorted out, Tom moved in. He

got on well with both girls. They cooked his dinner of an evening and supplied detergent for the washing machine but Tom would rarely pay them.

Shortly before Shaunagh went on a package holiday to Greece Sharon said to her, 'Tom is always on that telephone. What he's doing is phoning up people from a radio show chatline and sometimes he's on the phone for about half an hour at a time.' As the telephone was in Shaunagh's name she was quite concerned and replied, 'I'll speak to British Telecom tomorrow and get them to send the itemised bill in earlier just in case he decides to leave.'

A large white envelope arrived whilst Shaunagh was on holiday. Sharon, realising what it contained, opened it, and had the most terrible shock. There were many detailed sheets showing quite clearly that Tom had phoned people all over the UK. His calls amounted to five hundred pounds. Also, British Telecom asked for a large deposit immediately or the line would be cut off. When Tom came home from work Sharon showed him the bill. He shrugged his shoulders and said, 'I didn't realise the calls would be that much. I'll just have to pay Shaunagh so much a month.'

Sharon returned from work the following evening and as time went by, she began to wonder where Tom was. Around 9 p.m. she became very suspicious and went upstairs into his room. She looked around her and noticed all the surface tops were clear and there were no possessions lying on the floor. She opened the wardrobe door to find Tom's clothes missing. She looked through all the drawers and these too were empty. He had quite obviously moved out. As he had left no note or cheque she decided he was not going to pay his share of the bill. Sharon was unable to pay the large deposit British Telecom wanted and the phone was cut off a few days later. She told me of the situation but there was nothing I could do either.

I spoke to Shaunagh in her office the Monday after her return from holiday. I asked, 'How are you, and what's happening with the telephone?' She replied, 'I had just got my suitcase inside the street door when Sharon pounced on me and told me Tom had gone and she showed me the telephone bill. I couldn't believe it. I felt so ill I went up the pub with Sharon and got myself drunk.' 'How are you now?' I asked. She replied, 'I've phoned British Telecom and I've arranged to pay them eighty pounds a month for the next six months and I'll have to pay them for putting the phone back on, but this time I'm having incoming calls only so no one will be able to dial out. I'm pissed off.'

As I was concerned about the situation I phoned Shaunagh in her office two days later. This time it was the old Shaunagh. When I asked how she was feeling she said, 'I'm grand now.

It's only money after all.' I said, 'If that had happened to me I'd be as miserable as sin for about a fortnight.'

A few weeks later Shaunagh saw Tom in a pub. She went over to him and said, 'Thanks for leaving me a five hundred pound telephone bill. Can I have some money off you?' Tom replied, 'I'll come to the house next Friday and I'll give you all I can.' This he did, and gave Shaunagh two hundred pounds. After his visit no more was seen of Tom until Shaunagh went home to Derry for Christmas. She was walking down a street one evening and Tom drove past her in a car. He stopped and offered her a lift, which she accepted. On her return to London she told me of their meeting. I asked, 'Didn't you have a good old go at him and try to get your three hundred pounds back? If that had been me I'd have told him to give me fifty pounds out of his wallet. What did you do?' She replied, 'I'd completely forgotten all about the telephone bill and we just talked about our families and friends and that was all that was said.'

Shaunagh had to pay the remainder of the bill and a further eighty pounds for the reconnection.

Shaunagh knew I was writing this book. I said to her, 'I read in the paper the other day that a new author got a sixty thousand pound advance from her publisher. If that happens to me I'll take you out to dinner.' She replied, 'You are going to get all that money and that's all you're going to give me?'

1990

June

June was forty years old. I was forty-five. We met through a social club. We also met a lady called Maureen, aged forty-six, through the same social club and we would go out in a threesome most weekends. June lived in a large bedsit in Swiss Cottage and was unemployed but had a wealthy mother who gave her a generous weekly allowance. June had an American boyfriend called John who was aged thirty-five.

June had a long-standing friendship with an American called John. Every two years John would come to London and visit June and on his return home they would correspond. During his last visit John asked June to marry him. She took her time considering his proposal and finally agreed just before he returned to the States.

One evening at dinner June told me she was sorting out her affairs and would be leaving for the US within a few weeks. She said she was going to marry John in the United States and they would make their home there.

June spoke glowingly of her fiancé and told me he had a limp because he had tried to commit suicide but had failed. She said he put a loaded rifle barrel in to his mouth and pulled the trigger but missed his target and had been rushed to hospital where he underwent emergency surgery. The surgery saved his life but he was left paralysed down his left side.

June told me how unfair life had been to John. His father was trying to have him committed to a mental institution and the US authorities had stopped him from his studies at university where he had been hoping to qualify as a doctor. June said they wouldn't even allow him to be a pharmacist.

I didn't share June's optimism with this relationship and told her so but she had made up her mind and had bought an expensive lilac suit as her wedding outfit. Unable to dissuade her I advised, 'Don't have any guns in the house, June, because the last time he flipped his lid he missed at very close range and if he does it again, you never know, he might hit you.'

I spoke to June on the telephone a few days before she left for the States and John, but she didn't write to me as she had promised and to date I have heard nothing more from her.

1990

Maureen

Maureen was a forty-six-year-old divorcee who didn't look her years. We met through a social club. We also met a lady called June, aged forty, through the same club and we would go out in a threesome most weekends. I was forty-five.

Maureen was in her twenties when she took advantage of the ten pound assisted boat passage to Australia which was available in the Sixties if you agreed to settle there for at least two years.

On her arrival in Sydney, Maureen lived in an immigrants' hostel but soon found herself furnished accommodation where she had her own room and shared a kitchen/diner, bathroom and garden with three other tenants. Each tenant had their own small electric cooker in the kitchen/diner.

One Saturday afternoon Maureen decided to have dinner. She switched on her cooker, put a pie in the oven and placed a saucepan of potatoes on the sole electric burner. As soon as the water began to simmer she returned to her room. Ten minutes later she checked to see how her food was progressing. To her annoyance she found her potatoes had been replaced by a large pot of stew. Maureen removed the offending vessel and returned her saucepan to the burner. On her next visit to the kitchen Maureen again found the stewpot sitting on her oven ring. This time she lost her temper. She grabbed both handles of the stewpot and threw it up the back garden, once more placing her saucepan of potatoes on to her cooker.

Later that afternoon Maureen heard a knock on her door. She opened it to see a blond young man winking and smiling at her with the girl from upstairs standing behind him. He gave Maureen a good telling-off about the stewpot but all the time smiling at her and winking furiously. Maureen stood in the doorway quietly listening to this odd tirade and simply closed the door when he'd finished.

There were no further incidents in the kitchen.

Maureen lived in Australia for six years before returning to the UK.

1990

The Car Crash

It was an icy winter's day and I was returning home after shopping in St James' Street, Walthamstow. I saw a black man driving a blue car turn right into the main road at the bottom of the High Street, attempting to squeeze in to the oncoming traffic. He drove into a huge patch of ice and lost control of his vehicle, spinning around and around in ever-widening circles. A red car, also driven by a black man but with a slightly paler complexion, was travelling towards the blue car but stopped when the driver saw the other's difficulties. The blue car eventually hit the red one, creating a large dent in its right wing. As I had experienced a car crash myself I knew the problems you could encounter with insurance policies. I crossed the road and said to the driver of the red car, 'I saw exactly what happened here and if you need a witness I'll back you.' He thanked me and made a note of my name and address.

I returned to the pavement and stood beside a black woman as we watched the two men separate the cars. She said to me, 'Why did you pick on the black man?' I replied, 'Well, he hit the red car. The other feller didn't do anything wrong.' She said, 'Yes, okay, but it wasn't the black man's fault, it was an accident.' I didn't reply further but as I walked away I thought, 'Both those men were black. The one I helped obviously had some white in him so surely the black woman was being racist? And as for the comment, "It was an accident," if it hadn't been we should have called the police and reported a case of damage by criminal intent.'

1990

Old Bill

Bill was a widower aged seventy-six. He had developed gangrene in his right leg and it had been amputated. He was confined to a wheelchair and lived in an old people's home as he was unable to look after himself. I was forty-five.

The first time I saw Bill he was sitting in a wheelchair in the lounge window of an old people's home. I felt very sorry for him. As I passed him daily I eventually smiled and waved at him, and he waved back at me. We progressed to talking to each other in mime. One day he mouthed, 'Would you like to come in for a cup of tea?' I nodded in reply. I walked up the pathway to the main entrance and rang the doorbell. The matron answered. I said, 'I'd like to see the old man who sits in the window but I don't know which flat he lives in.' She replied, 'That's Bill. Come in and I'll take you to him.' I followed her and she continued, 'He says every time you smile and wave at him you make his day.' Bill and I became very good friends and I would frequently stop for tea and a chat.

Soon other passers-by did the same. Bill said to me, 'When I sit in that window everyone waves to me and they all come in to see me. I've put this place on the map. Nobody else has the visitors I have.'

A year later I moved to another town and only passed the Home occasionally. Several times I noticed Bill was missing from the window and I couldn't find him in his flat either. Eventually I rang the main doorbell. I spoke to the matron again. I asked, 'Is everything alright with Bill? I haven't seen him for ages.' She replied, 'I'm very sorry, but Bill passed away a few months ago. He developed gangrene in his left leg and the doctors said if he didn't have it amputated he would die. Bill wouldn't have the leg off because he thought he'd be too much trouble for people.'

1992

Cheryl

I met Cheryl through a social club for single women. The club supplied names, telephone numbers and the ages of unattached females seeking friends. I contacted Cheryl and we decided to meet in a pub central to both of us. We exchanged descriptions. She was forty. I was forty-seven.

Cheryl and I sat at a table in the pub of our choice one Friday evening. For the first hour I kept the conversation going with Cheryl just replying, 'Yes' or 'No'. She downed her second glass of wine and began to unwind. She told me, 'I'm divorced from my husband and I have a teenage daughter at school. I had a very bad marriage. My husband was always violent towards me. He pushed me down the stairs when I was expecting Joanne. Then he had an affair with my sister and ran off with her. I divorced him soon after that and now he's married to my sister and they also have a daughter. They live across the road from me so I see them every day but we never speak. I'm not sure what the relationship is with the children. I suppose Joanne is a cousin and also a stepsister.'

She sipped her third drink and continued, 'I've been very unlucky with my health. I had to have a mastectomy a few years ago and now I only have one breast. I haven't got very much money either. I have rent to pay and Joanne to support.'

We spent the remainder of the evening politely talking about life in general but I was relieved when it was closing time as I found her life story far too bizarre to contemplate. We parted on friendly terms but we did not make any arrangements to see each other again.

1992

Ide

Ide was a twenty-three-year-old Irish nurse who shared a furnished house for a short time with my friend Shaunagh, also aged twenty-three. Both girls frequented the Irish pub in Leytonstone where they had many friends. There was a lodging house next door to the pub known as 'The Maze'. Several Irishmen lived there. I was forty-seven.

Ide liked to have a good drink of a weekend and would often go to the Irish pub in Leytonstone with Shaunagh.

One Saturday Ide spent the evening supping pint after pint of beer until she was drunk. At closing time she was in no fit condition to travel so her friends arranged for her to share a bed with one of their drinking partners, an Irishman called Terry, who lived in the house next door. He was also the worse for wear and it was clear they would only sleep together.

Unfortunately Ide must have downed some twenty pints, which resulted in Terry waking on the Sunday morning to discover she had wet the bed. He left the still sleeping Ide and had a hot shower in the communal bathroom but he was unable to keep his experience secret and soon half the regulars of the pub knew of Ide's mishap. Shaunagh eventually heard the story and told me on the understanding that I wouldn't repeat it.

1992

Ali

Ali was thirty-four. I was forty-eight when we met. He was a political refugee living in London because he refused to speak Turkish and attend a mosque in his native Turkey as he was Kurdish and a Christian. The Turkish government imprisoned him for one year for this crime. He worked as a presser in a London factory. We dated for three years. Our age gap did not worry either one of us.

Ali and I met on Boxing Day 1992 as I walked to a Pakistani supermarket at the top of Walthamstow High Street. He was standing idly at the traffic lights as I passed by and he spoke to me. He asked, 'Me and you go for coffee?' I looked round at him and replied, 'No, thank you. I'm going shopping.' He asked, 'Me help you?' As it would soon be the New Year and I was out to have some fun I took a good look at him. I saw he was smartly dressed in a heavy tracksuit and quite handsome, so I said, 'Okay.' I continued walking and Ali followed me. I picked up one of the wire baskets outside the store and he took it from me. We walked slowly through the aisles as I filled the basket he was carrying.

My shopping complete I said to Ali, 'I'm going home now.' He asked, 'Me come with you?' I replied, 'There are no buses today and it's a twenty minute walk to where I live. You can only come in for a quick coffee anyway, so do you still want to come with me?' He replied, 'Okay, no problem.' We walked towards my home with Ali now carrying my large blue shopping bag. We chatted as we walked, exchanging names and telling each other our circumstances. Ali's spoken English was very poor. I discovered he knew a lot of words but he was unable to form sentences.

I let him into the empty furnished house I lived in and unlocked my flatlet door. He sat down on my two-seater settee and I made him a coffee. When he had finished I said, 'Will you go now please?' He replied, 'Okay. Give me telephone number,' which I did, and he left the house.

Ali phoned me a few days later and it was the start of a long relationship. We found we both had the same sense of humour and this made up for our lack of verbal communication. As time went by his English improved. In the beginning he would phone and say, 'This me come?' and I would understand him to mean 'Shall I come round tonight?' He slowly progressed to saying, 'Me see you eight o'clock today?'

Ali had a lot of Turkish and Kurdish friends in London and he would spend hours drinking Turkish coffee and talking, drinking whisky and talking, or playing cards and gambling all night. After one of his whisky and talking sessions he decided to spend the rest of the night with me. He came to my flatlet by minicab at one thirty in the morning and told the driver to wait. He tapped on my downstairs front room window, which was my lounge/bedroom, but unfortunately I was fast asleep and didn't hear him. He continued tapping but I didn't wake up. He pressed the various doorbells in the porch but no one answered him and he was forced to return to the minicab and have the driver take him home.

Fifteen months into our relationship it was early March and cold with dark evenings. As I sat in my flatlet I began to think to myself, 'Where is Ali? I haven't heard from him for over a week and that's very unusual.' A few days passed with still no contact from Ali. On the Friday evening at approximately seven thirty the upstairs communal telephone rang. I ran up the stairs and answered it. A foreign voice said, 'Sylvia?' I replied, 'Yes'. He said, 'Ali'. I said, 'Yes'. He said, 'Ali. Car crash. Whipps Cross Hospital. Understand?' My heart was pounding as I replied, 'Yes, okay, understand.' The stranger was only able to repeat the same few words so I finished the call. I ran down the stairs with my thoughts racing. I tried not to panic. I thought, 'Find out where he is and how he is and get to Whipps Cross Hospital at top speed.' I put my shoes on and ran up the stairs with some coins and called Directory Enquiries for the hospital telephone number.

A member of staff looked down the admission list and said, 'Mr Sundu is on "S" ward. Would you like me to put you through?' I replied, 'Yes please.' A few seconds later I spoke to the sister on Ali's ward. I said, 'I understand you have Ali Sundu with you?' She replied, 'Yes, I have. He had his operation yesterday.' My heart pounded even faster and I said, 'Operation! Is he alright?' She replied, 'Yes, of course.' I asked, 'Can I see him this evening?' She replied, 'Yes, but visiting hours finish at eight thirty.'

I raced down the stairs and found another coin and phoned for a minicab, telling them it was urgent. Twenty minutes later I was in the hospital Reception. I had to wait several nerve-wracking minutes for the receptionist to finish a telephone call. Eventually she gave me the directions to 'S' ward. I ran through the roadways of the vast hospital thinking to myself 'That nurse said visiting hours finished at 8:30 and I don't know what the time is.' I soon got lost but fortunately another nurse sent me in the right direction and I finally found 'S' ward. As I hurried along the corridor I saw Ali lying in the second bed on the left. I calmed down completely when he saw me and smiled.

I sat down on the chair beside him and held his hand. He tried to tell me what had happened in his broken English but I didn't fully understand him. A middle-aged woman visitor sitting in the chair by the next bed interrupted and said, 'I'm here every day seeing my husband and I saw Ali when he came in. I couldn't miss overhearing so I can give you all the details.' I said, 'I would be very pleased if you would.' She continued, 'The police came with an an interpreter and through the interpreter Ali said he'd been crossing the road to catch the bus to take him to work and a woman driver in a red car drove in to him. She stopped and reversed and drove in to him again. Then she drove away. Ali said he thought his leg was shattered so he crawled out of the road onto the pavement. The bus driver saw what happened and called the police and an ambulance and Ali has been here for ten days now. Before he had his operation the doctor got the interpreter back and he told Ali he had to have two metal splints put into the side of his right leg and one behind his right knee. Then he'll be on crutches for a while and in two years' time he'll have to have another operation to take the metal splints out.' I asked, 'He will be alright again won't he?' She replied, 'Yes, of course he will but it's going to take time.' I thanked her and turned back to Ali.

Ali said to me, 'Me no like hospital. Me no like operation. Me no like nurses. Me no like food.

Me hot. Me pain. Me cry.' By this time I realised there was nothing seriously wrong with him and I thought to myself, 'You big baby! I've just had the shock of my life thinking you were in some terrible car crash and had to have a life-saving operation and here you are with a busted leg!'

I went to see Ali every day while he was in hospital and I discovered that visitors could see patients from 11 a.m. until nine thirty at night as long as they did not hinder the nurses. So I need not have rushed that first evening. Ali was always smiling and joking with the other patients and visiting times were fun. He was discharged from hospital two weeks later and he spent the following six months on crutches. The surgeon did an excellent job on him and Ali made a complete recovery.

The police were unable to trace the woman driver in the accident and she never came forward. Also, despite seeing a solicitor, Ali was unable to get any type of compensation. He told me the solicitor was going to give him his bill. Ali said, 'Me run over, me operation, me sick, me no work and me pay solicitor?' Fortunately his solicitor decided to waive his charges.

My opinion of the accident was that possibly it was Ali's fault. He had been crossing the road to catch the bus to take him to work and in his haste he may have looked left instead of right and stepped out in front of the oncoming car.

1992

Paul C

Paul was thirty-nine. I was forty-seven. We met at a disco. He was a ladies' hairdresser. Unfortunately, although I liked him I found him to be very effeminate. I didn't like his slightly bouffant, permed hairdo and our conversation was similar to that I would have with one of my girlfriends and not that of a man and woman. We went out together once.

Paul owned a very large house in Hornsey. He lived on the ground floor and let all the other rooms out, earning himself five hundred pounds a week in rents from his tenants. I asked him, 'Don't you ever have any trouble being a landlord?' He replied, 'When I see everyone we just say "hello" or "goodnight" and they pay their rent and that's the end of it, but I did have a man commit suicide in one of my rooms upstairs. I smelt gas outside his door and as I couldn't get an answer from him I got the keys and went in. I found him dead in bed with a plastic bag over his head with a tube inside connected to the gas oven. I called the police and they had him taken away but it was a grisly experience for me.'

Paul told me, 'I did have my own unisex hairdressing salon until recently. I employed a male hairdresser and let him work without cards and then he decided to leave and work for someone else and he took half my customers with him. He cost me about three hundred pounds a week. As he ruined my business for me I told the tax people he'd been working full-time, claiming housing benefit and unemployment pay, and I suppose he's going to have to repay the authorities. If he hadn't taken my customers away I would have let him go without causing any trouble.'

1992

The Grope

I was aged forty-seven.

Every Monday evening for several months I went to an over-twenty-five's disco in Enfield with a group of girlfriends. The men were all very attractive and aged from thirty-five upwards. My girlfriends and I were frequently asked to dance but as soon as the DJ played a series of slow numbers the lights would go down and all my dancing partners expected me to be a willing party to an instant embrace and necking session and they all seemed surprised at my reluctance.

One Monday evening I was asked to dance during the slow numbers by a foreign man I decided was French and aged about thirty-six. He followed me on to the floor and held me very tightly as we danced. His hands wandered up and down my back and over my rear. He buried his face in my neck and started to kiss me whilst breathing heavily in my right ear. We had known each other for approximately twenty seconds and I didn't like his attentions at all. I broke free of his caresses and I said to him, 'I said yes to a dance, not a grope.' He didn't reply but we started dancing in a normal manner. When the record had finished I said, 'Thank you' to my partner and returned to my table.

Approximately fifteen minutes later my Frenchman came up to me. He said, 'I am sorry for our dancing. Please forgive me.'

1992

Jean

Jean was thirty years old and a colleague of Pat, aged forty-eight. Pat was a friend and neighbour of Nancy, aged forty. I was a friend of both Pat and Nancy. I was aged forty-seven.

I went to see Nancy one Wednesday afternoon for our usual cup of tea and gossip. We settled down with our mugs and she said to me, 'Pat has taken in a lodger called Jean. She's one of her workmates and she's just finished living with a boyfriend and didn't have anywhere else to go. Pat said she's really easy to get on with and it's nice to have some company so Jean can live there indefinitely. Apparently Jean lived with her boyfriend for three years and all they did was argue. They're still going to see each other occasionally as friends, but she's on the look out for someone else.'

Jean joined the three of us on our weekly date at a local disco.

I continued seeing Nancy on a Wednesday

afternoon. A few months later she said to me, 'I've got some really juicy gossip! Jean has brilliantly got herself pregnant by her ex-boyfriend! She's going to have the baby and her and her ex are going to rent a house in the country and live together with the child. I think they're both crazy. If I had been Jean I would not have got myself pregnant with someone I'd finished with, and to go back and live with a boyfriend I didn't get on with at all for the sake of the baby is stupid. It will never work.'

Eighteen months later Jean left her boyfriend and started life anew in London with her daughter.

1992

The Borrower

I was forty-seven and staying with my parents. Our visitor was aged about thirty.

One winter's night the street doorbell rang. I went to answer it, followed by my elderly father, as it was a late hour to have a caller. I opened the door to see a young black man wearing a duffle jacket. He said, 'I'm really sorry to disturb you and I don't like ringing on your door but I'm lodging at No. 58 and I've shut myself out. I've left my keys in my room with my money and no one is in so I can't get in to the house. Could you please lend me two pounds fifty so I can get a Travelcard because I haven't got any cash on me and I'm on the night shift at Fords of Dagenham. I'll give it back to you tomorrow evening.'

I felt very sorry for him and replied, 'Wait a minute and I'll get my purse,' and shut the door. My father asked me, 'Do you know this bloke?' I replied, 'No, but I think I can help a neighbour in trouble.' He said, 'You must be crazy. You'll never see him again.' I ignored my father's protests and returned to the street door with three one pound coins and gave them to the black man. He said, 'Thank you very much.' I asked, 'You will give this back to me?' He replied, 'Yes, of course. I'll put it in an envelope tomorrow and post it through your letterbox.' I closed the door. My father said, 'You amaze me. You won't see that feller or your three pounds ever again.'

Two nights passed without the return of my money and on the third evening I began to wonder if my father had been right. It also occurred to me if the black man lived at No. 58 why didn't he knock on No. 56 or No. 54, as we were No. 46 and some distance away from him. I determined to find out. I donned my outdoor clothing and knocked on No. 58. An old lady opened the door. I asked her, 'Can I speak to your lodger please?' She replied, 'I haven't got any lodgers, dear. I live here all by myself.' I told her what had happened. She said, 'Oh, you silly thing. You won't see your money now.'

1992

Roogie and James

I shared a furnished house owned by a Nigerian family. The two other tenants were a woman called Roogie, aged thirty-two, from the Gambia, and James, aged thirty, a big, burly Irishman with sparkling blue eyes and soft blond curls. I was forty-seven.

I found living with Roogie and James to be extremely unpleasant. I considered them to be odd because they didn't like conversation. When they returned from work in the evening it was perfectly alright to say 'Good evening' and tell them of any telephone messages but they did not like to talk further. We shared a TV lounge and I was expected to sit in total silence all evening whilst we watched the programmes. At weekends the three of us would attend to our various jobs without saying any more than 'Good morning' and my attempts at chatter would upset them. Unless it was relevant, conversation was not allowed.

Roogie would have a bath every evening. She would wrap a towel around her waist and walk about the house topless. If she met James or me she would say 'Excuse me,' and cover her bare bosom with her arm.

James was extremely bad-tempered. If either Roogie or I asked him to fix something he would do the job, usually very minor, but it would anger him. Both Roogie and James thought it quite normal to have a flaming row, calling each other names, then three hours later resume friendly terms as though nothing had happened.

We soon found we had a cat problem. If we left the house without shutting all the downstairs windows we would return to find our black dustbin-bag of rubbish scattered over the kitchen floor. Sometimes the adjoining bathroom door was ajar and we would arrive in time to see a fat tabby cat running along the side of the bath, making dirty footprints, as he escaped through the small top louvre. We tried securing the house before leaving but frequently we would be at home and the cat would still manage to rummage through our refuse. This happened so many times James said, 'If I ever get my hands on that blighter I'll murder him.'

I was hanging out my washing one Saturday morning. I was startled to see our tabby cat laying flat on his back with his paws in the air underneath a large bush at the back of the garden. He was quite obviously dead. I went into the house and told Roogie. She said to me, 'James killed that cat.' I said, 'You must be joking!' She replied, 'No. Didn't you hear doors banging last night and a cat screaming?' I thought for a moment and replied, 'Yes, I did but I thought it was a cat fight.' Roogie said, 'No, it wasn't. James caught the cat and killed it.' I could not believe this and asked her, 'Did you see him do it?' 'Yes,' she replied. When I saw James I asked him, 'Did you kill the cat?' He replied, 'No,' and walked away from me. I thought about the situation and concluded that James was probably quite skilled at killing chickens, rabbits and possibly other small animals as he had been brought up in the countryside of Ireland. Also the cat fight I thought I'd heard had only lasted two minutes, and how often do they kill each other? I decided Roogie had told me the truth. When I recovered from the shock I said to her, 'That certainly solves our cat problem, doesn't it!'

Although I disliked the eerie atmosphere, I lived in the house for seven months before moving because I was unemployed and the social services had not sorted out my housing benefit. I didn't trust them not to get confused if I changed addresses. Finally I could stand no more of the silent Roogie and James and found myself other accommodation. I informed the authorities. To my great relief I soon received a large cheque covering my oustanding rent.

Paul

Paul was aged thirty. He lived in a bedsit in the furnished house we both shared. I was forty-eight.

Paul knocked on my door one evening, holding a striped shirt in his hands. He asked, 'Sylvia, could you repair the cuffs on this shirt for me please?' I replied, 'Come in and sit down but make sure you leave the door wide open.' I examined the article and said, 'All this needs is just a bit of gathering then about ten minutes' machining. It's quite a simple job so I'll do it for you.' He told me how he had tried to shorten the sleeves by cutting the material above the cuffs but had been unable to finish the work. It was some ten minutes later that he said in a very aggrieved tone, 'I don't see why I should leave the door open, Sylvia. It's not as though I'm going to pounce on you.' I laughed and replied, 'I was only joking, Paul.'

I successfully repaired his shirt and received an expensive box of white chocolates in return.

1993

The Flower Seller

For twenty years he sold flowers from a stall outside our local hospital. He was approximately forty years old. I was forty-eight.

As I crossed the High Street I noticed the flower seller riding past on his bicycle. I returned his 'Hello' and continued on my way. Thirty yards further down the street I heard the 'ting ting' of a bell. I turned to see the flower seller straddling his stationary bike with his left leg over the crossbar. Encouraged by my smile he asked, 'Can I take you for a cup of tea?'

I declined his offer.

1993

Ron, Bill and Richard

Next door to my furnished accommodation lived an elderly widower and his two sons. Ron, the father, was sixty-seven, his eldest son, Bill, was thirty-eight, and his youngest son, Richard, was thirty. Their house was rented and they did not keep it very clean. I was forty-eight.

I was walking home with my shopping one summer's afternoon when Richard suddenly appeared beside me. 'Have you got twenty-nine pence?' he asked. I delved into my purse and gave him the money. I lived next door to him for four years but he did not repay me.

I was woken one Sunday morning at approximately 1.45 a.m. by Ron and one of the neighbours returning home drunk from their Saturday night out at the local club. Ron was fumbling in his pockets for his street door key but was unable to find it. By now his friend was nearing his own house a few doors away. Ron yelled to him, 'I've forgotten me fucking key!' Ron staggered up his pathway. He pounded his fists on the door and bellowed through the letterbox until one of his sons let him in. He stumbled into his hallway shouting to his waiting friend, 'I'm alright now mate,' slamming the street door behind him.

I repeated Ron's escapade to Lynne, who lived in the flat adjacent to mine, and she said, 'The two brothers had a fight in their kitchen the other Sunday morning over a bit of bacon. Apparently Richard had nicked Bill's bacon and Bill punched him on the nose. I heard Richard shout, "He's broken me fucking nose again," and the old boy said, "Stop this fighting, you two are supposed to be brothers."'

Bill was divorced and his wife had custody of their three young children. He had a long-term girlfriend who lived with him at weekends. My neighbour, Rene, whose bedroom adjoined Bill's, said to me, 'When they have sex you can hear her howling through the wall.'

Lynne's live-in boyfriend, Dave, said to me, 'One Saturday morning I was sitting in the back garden with one of me mates and Bill and his girlfriend had their bedroom window open and you could hear her groaning away louder and louder and when she had her orgasm me mate clapped his hands and cheered.'

1993

Denise

Denise was thirty-nine and the divorced mother of two teenagers. She lived in the next street to Jenny H and we all became friends.

Denise began dating her neighbour Derek who lived in a house four doors away from her. Two weeks in to their romance they returned to Denise's home after spending the evening in their local pub. They became very amorous and had sex together, resulting in Derek sharing Denise's double bed for the night. The following morning he said to her, 'Don't get carried away by all of this. I really don't want anything serious.' Denise replied, 'Okay,' but found she liked him and secretly hoped a long-term relationship would develop.

They continued seeing one another and had an affair that lasted several months until they had a flaming row. After this neither one telephoned the other and they would pass each other in the street. Denise coped quite well with this behaviour and was optimistic that Derek would eventually relent and contact her again.

One Sunday morning Denise saw Derek parking his car with an unknown blonde sitting in the passenger seat. She watched as he picked up the woman's suitcase and led her into his house. Denise became very upset and realised Derek had replaced her. As time went by her mood changed to fury and she decided to pay him a visit. She knocked on his street door. Some minutes passed before he opened it, wearing a dressing gown. As it was still daylight Denise was consumed with rage, 'I want to know what's going on here you bastard,' she yelled as she pushed past Derek and stormed down the hallway. She discovered the blonde sitting in the lounge sipping a cup of tea, also wearing a dressing gown. It was quite clear to Denise that they were lovers. She screamed at Derek, 'Oh, wasn't I good enough for you then? Didn't you like the way I did it? Does this slag know you've been bonking me for the last few months? How long has this been going on, you creep?' Denise continued her tirade whilst Derek quietly listened. The blonde sipped her tea, trying to ignore the situation. When Denise finally paused for breath Derek said, 'I told you from the very beginning that I didn't want anything serious with you.' Denise screamed in temper and left the house, slamming the street door behind her.

Denise did not calm down. She became more and more angry. After a sleepless night, she planned her revenge. She carried her lawnmower along the pavement and used all her strength to lift it high into the air. Then she let it fall on to the roof of Derek's car, causing an enormous dent. She removed his doorkey from her chain and walked around the car scratching the paintwork. Her deed completed she punched a hole through one of the small panes of glass in Derek's street door, throwing the key into the hallway.

Derek did nothing in retaliation to Denise. He saw the condition of his car when he returned from work and spoke to a neighbour who had witnessed the act but he did not report the matter to the police. He paid a garage to repair the damage and he replaced the broken glass in his door. His affair with the blonde didn't last but he made no further contact with Denise.

1993

Marion

Marion was fifty-five. I was forty-eight. I posted a householdware catalogue through her street door. We met when I returned to collect it.

I rang Marion's street doorbell to collect my catalogue. I saw her shadow through the frosted glass as she walked into her hallway. She called out 'Who is it?' I replied, 'It's Sylvia from Betterware.' 'Oh that's alright then,' she said and opened the door to me saying, 'I'm Marion. Would you like to come in? There are a few bits and pieces I would like.'

I followed Marion into her lounge and I saw she was using walking sticks and wearing a large scarf over her head. She pointed to an armchair and said, 'If you'd like to sit down there I'll write out my order.' She asked, 'Are you doing this in your spare time?' I replied, 'No. I'm unemployed and I'm trying to find some type of job.' She said, 'I'm off sick.' I said, 'I hope it isn't anything serious.' She replied, 'I'm afraid it is. I've got cancer.' I said, 'God, that's terrible!' She said, 'I started off with breast cancer and I've had a breast removed. Then a few weeks ago I had a check-up and the doctors told me the cancer has spread all over my back. I've got to go to hospital for further treatment next week.' I said, 'Well, you must be in with a chance otherwise they wouldn't be treating you.' Marion smiled and said, 'That would be lovely, wouldn't it?' and passed me the completed form.

Ten days later I returned to Marion's house with the various products she had requested. We settled in her lounge. I asked her, 'How did you get on at the hospital?' She replied, 'Unfortunately the doctors told me the cancer has spread too far and they can't do any more for me.' I said, 'I'm sorry.' She replied, 'Oh, don't be. It's only one of life's little battles.' I asked, 'Aren't you upset about it?' She replied, 'Not really. I've got used to things now and I've always tried to live my life to the full. I know that I'm dying but there's nothing anyone can do about it. I'm in a lot of pain at the moment but the hospital said they'd sort that out for me so I'll just have to take things as they come.' She was pleased with her purchases and continued talking to me. She said, 'I spent three years teaching in New Zealand and then I got on a train and travelled from one side of Canada to the other. So I have lived quite a lot and I've always had enough money to have the things I wanted.' She paused for a while. I asked her, 'Is there anything I can do for you?' She thought for a moment and said 'Would you mind doing my washing up? I just can't manage to stand that long. And I've got a few letters I'd like posted.' I was pleased to help her and also gave the kitchen a quick clean. I said, 'I could pop in once a week to see if you want anything.' She replied, 'Please do. I'll probably have more letters to post.' She gave me several stamped envelopes and I left her house.

A week later I saw an elderly lady at Marion's street door. I walked up the pathway and said, 'I've come to see how Marion is.' She replied, 'I was doing the same thing dear, and I've just rung the bell.' Marion welcomed us. I discovered the friend was named Miriam and they had both worked together as schoolteachers. We chatted until Marion finally said, 'I'm sorry but I'm very tired now. If you wouldn't mind going. I usually have a nap about this time.' Miriam said, 'Don't worry dear, we understand.'

A few days later I rang Marion's doorbell. As there was no answer I shouted through the letterbox. She called from her upstairs bedroom, 'I haven't got anything I want you to do today. I'm in bed trying to have a sleep and I'm too tired to talk to you but thank you for the visit.'

The following week I went to see Marion. Despite my efforts I could get no reply. Her next door neighbour saw me standing in the porch and came out to speak to me. She asked, 'Are you looking for Marion?' I replied, 'Yes, I am. I wanted to know how she was getting on.' The neighbour replied, 'I'm sorry to give you bad news but she died last Friday.'

Marion's neighbour, Anne, and I both remarked how calmly Marion had taken her illness. Anne said to me, 'When Marion was first diagnosed as having breast cancer the doctors wanted to operate immediately but she wouldn't let them. Two months went by before she agreed and I think that delay probably cost her her life because soon after the operation she was told the cancer had spread to her back. Then she was eventually told there was no hope.' I said, 'I think it's a terrible shame. She was such a brave woman.' Anne replied, 'My twenty-year-old son did his best to look after her. Marion said to him, "Please don't be sad because I'm not." She told him to take a cutting from her fuchsia plant in the front garden as something for him to remember her by.' I said, 'I used to knock on her door occasionally to see if she needed any help and she always used walking sticks. The cancer must have affected her legs as well.' Anne replied, 'That's not right. Didn't you know she was handicapped and she had walking sticks to help her walk? She also gave that as the reason why she never married. She said she felt it was very unfair for her to marry a man with her disability so she never let any man get close to her.'

1994

Miriam

Miriam was an elderly lady of eighty-seven years and in robust good health. We became acquainted whilst visiting a mutual friend dying of cancer. I was forty-nine.

I always stopped to talk to Miriam when I saw her in the street. She was usually busy going to and from the local school where she taught part-time, or on a shopping trip. She was very religious and wore a brooch inscribed 'JESUS' on her coat.

As I strolled through the park one afternoon I met Miriam. She seemed very downcast and I asked her what was wrong. She replied, 'I was walking down Forest Drive about a week ago when a schoolboy, and he was only about ten dear, grabbed my handbag and ran off with it. I couldn't possibly chase after him and I was so shocked that this type of thing could happen in broad daylight, especially from a child. I went to the police and they were wonderful but they didn't hold out much hope of ever getting my handbag back again. It had my purse in it with a little bit of money, my house keys and my appointment card with the hospital. I thought I'd better change my keys and that cost me seventy-six pounds. Then I bought myself another handbag and purse and that cost me twenty pounds, and I had to telephone the hospital because I couldn't remember when my appointment was. Then two days later I had a call from the police. They said they'd found my handbag with everything in it except the money in my purse.'

Although I sympathised with her I thought it would have been a lot cheaper if she had waited a few days before replacing anything.

1994

Virginia's Mugging

Mr Manford was an elderly Jewish man and my landlord. He owned sixteen furnished houses. He divided each house into various-sized flats and let them out. Virginia was an attractive Jewish woman aged fifty-six whom he employed to manage his properties. She lived rent-free in one of his apartments. I was forty-nine.

Every fourth Friday Virginia collected the rents on Mr Manford's properties. She usually arrived shortly after 11 a.m. at the house I shared.

On one such Friday morning I was watching television in my downstairs front room. Virginia knocked on my door for my cheque and slowly worked her way through the various apartments. She hurried down the pathway when she had finished. A few minutes later I heard a sudden squeal of brakes and looked out of my bay window expecting to see some type of accident. I saw Virginia sitting in the driving seat of her car, looking straight ahead, with a blue Ford alongside her. As the scene was peaceful I returned to my TV.

Around lunchtime the communal telephone rang. I raced up the stairs to answer it. Virginia spoke to me. She asked, 'Are you going to be in for the rest of the day, dear?' I replied, 'No, I'm going out in about half an hour.' She asked, 'Is Dave in downstairs?' I replied, 'Yes, he is. I'll get him for you.'

Dave knocked on my door. He said, 'Guess what's happened?' I replied, 'No, what?' He said, 'Virginia has just been mugged and it was right outside here.' I said, 'You're joking!' He said, 'No, I'm not! Apparently there were two fellers lying in wait for her. One had a car and pulled up beside her, blocking her inside her car, and the other bloke opened the passenger door and nicked all the money. They were both wearing balaclavas and Virginia didn't get their number plate so I reckon they've got away with it.' I asked, 'Now what's going to happen?' He replied, 'Virginia wants someone in the house because the street door lock has got to be changed. The villains got everything, all the money, all the cheques, all the keys. And it wasn't just the money from this house. She'd already collected the rents from four other houses as well.' We both giggled and waited for future developments.

Mr Manford came to the house in the afternoon and pinned a letter to the noticeboard in the downstairs hallway. It requested everyone to cancel any cheques they had left as payment for rent. He told us Virginia was quite well although a little shaken. A locksmith attended to the street door and Dave was given the new keys to hand to the other tenants as they returned home.

I thought about the situation and realised I had witnessed the beginning of the mugging but when I looked out of my window all had seemed well so I had turned away and missed the most crucial part. I decided, 'So much for my abilities as a sleuth.'

1994

Dr Shah

Dr Shah became my GP when I moved to another area in East London. He was happily married and the father of four children. He was a Sikh. Because of his religion he was not allowed to cut hair on any part of his body. His long, black hair was tucked inside a black turban and a black beard trickled past his chest. He was always dressed in black. He was thirty-four. I was forty-nine.

Dr Shah and I were on very friendly terms. Each time I visited him we would exchange pleasantries. On one of my visits he told me he owned two parrots, that the female had laid an egg, and as soon as the young parrot was old enough he intended housing him in a cage in his surgery. I looked around the room and noted the human skull on the shelf. I said, 'I've never known a doctor have a parrot in his surgery. Don't you think it's an odd thing to do?' 'No, not at all,' he replied, 'It will probably take my patients' minds off their problems.' 'Are you going to leave him on his own overnight?' I asked. 'No. I'll take him home at the end of my day.' he replied.

A few weeks passed before I found it necessary to pay Dr Shah another visit. I entered his surgery expecting to see a parrot in its cage. 'Where's your parrot?' I queried. 'Don't talk to me about my parrot!' he exclaimed. 'Why? What's happened?' I asked. He replied, 'I bought a very nice cage and hung it in my surgery. The following day I drove here with the parrot in my right hand. As I got out of the car I dropped my keys and the noise upset the parrot. He wriggled free out of my hand and the last time I saw him he was flying over the roof tops.'

On another visit to Dr Shah I sat in the waiting room while a five-year-old Indian girl was taken to see him. I was his next appointment. When I entered his surgery he said, 'Do you know I had two chocolates sitting on the side of my desk and that little brat picked up both of them and ate them!'

1994

Mrs Murphy

Mrs Murphy was an elderly Irish woman who lived in the next street to me. I became her cleaning lady, working every Friday morning from 10 a.m. until noon.

My neighbour Rene worked in a Pakistani supermarket in Leyton High Road. One morning Mrs Murphy went into the shop to place an ad in the window for a part-time cleaning lady. Rene wrote out the card then suddenly thought of me. She saw me later in the day and asked me if I was interested. I thought it was worth a try and phoned Mrs Murphy. An interview was arranged for the following evening at 6 p.m.

I knocked on Mrs Murphy's street door at the appropriate time. It was opened by May, her daughter, who ushered me into the front room where Mrs Murphy was sitting in an armchair.

I found out later that May was aged fifty-one,

divorced with no children, and an executive secretary in the City.

May proceeded to give me a grilling which I thought was more suitable for employing office staff and not for someone who was only going to use a vacuum cleaner and wash two floors. She told me they had a small poodle. I said, 'I'm not very good with animals and I'm nervous of dogs.' May pounced on this and added, 'Oh, we have a little cat too.' Mrs Murphy, who had been silently listening to our discussion, interrupted, 'I can easily keep the animals out of her way.' This did not placate May. She said, 'We do have other applicants to see. Thank you for coming and we'll let you know our decision in a few days' time.'

I walked home with the feeling that May found me totally unsuitable.

A few evenings later the communal telephone in the upper hallway rang. I rushed to answer it. A voice said, 'Hello, Sylvia. This is Mrs Murphy. I'm calling to see if you would like to be our cleaning lady?' I replied, 'Yes, I'd be delighted.' She said, 'We'll see you at 10 a.m. Friday then.'

The next morning I saw Rene and told her I'd got the job. She replied, 'I'm not surprised. I forgot to put the card in the window so you were their only applicant.'

1994

MRS MURPHY'S HOLIDAY

Mrs Murphy was an elderly Irish lady whose house I cleaned for two hours every Friday morning for three years. She was seventy-eight. I was forty-nine. Her fifty-one-year-old divorced daughter, May, lived at the family home with her parents. Mrs Murphy was the mother of seven adult children, all of whom were happily married except for May.

Mr Murphy was a semi-invalid and had been in poor health for some years and was almost bedridden, which meant that Mrs Murphy could never leave him for very long. She told me, 'When my husband retired I thought we would spend our old age visiting, but it was not to be.'

Sometimes I noticed Mrs Murphy was very down. She would frequently say to me, 'I could do with a good holiday and a complete break from this house but I can't leave Jack on his own with May working full-time as well.'

One Friday an excited Mrs Murphy said to

me, 'My daughter Ann and I are having a week's holiday in Dublin so I'm going to get a nice break after all. May is going to work shorter hours and take care of her father for me so I won't have to worry about Jack. This will be the first time in years that I've had a proper holiday.' I was very pleased for her despite her adding, 'We won't need you while I'm away, Sylvia.'

I noticed it was fine weather during her holiday and I thought she must be thoroughly enjoying herself, especially as she was visiting 'the old country'.

The week after her return I rang her doorbell and heard Prince, the poodle, barking away as usual, but Mr Murphy greeted me. I asked him, 'Where is Mrs Murphy?' He replied, 'Go in the front room and see.' I did as he said and saw her sitting in an armchair as white as a sheet, wearing her night clothes and looking very unwell. 'What happened to you?' I asked, 'And what about your holiday?' She replied, 'As soon as I got to the hotel I got sick and had to go to bed and the doctor was called. He said I either had a touch of food poisoning or a tummy bug, and I spent the entire week ill in bed. I was very very ill and when we came back I had to travel to and from the plane in a wheelchair. My eldest son met us at Heathrow and it was a great relief to get home. I was terribly disappointed and it's such a waste of money. The hotel alone cost me three hundred and sixty pounds.' She paused and sighed, 'Oh, well that's life, isn't it?'

Mrs Murphy slowly climbed the stairs to bed and I got on with the cleaning of the house. When I had finished she called me to her room. 'Here's your money, Sylvia,' she said and gave me my wages. She delved into her purse and held her hand out again, saying. 'And this is last week's money too.'

1994

Raf

Raf was forty-five and originated from Guyana. He ran two cut-price clothing stalls on the pavement outside a pub in Leyton High Road. I was forty-nine.

I would pass Raf's clothing stalls on my way to the shops and often stopped to see his latest ranges.

One Thursday I bought the local newspaper and was amazed to see an article about him on the front page. It stated that Raf was suing the pub for the rent he had paid them since trading there. The reason he made headline news was because he should not have paid any rent at all as the pavement is public property.

I saw Raf the following day and I said to him, 'I've been reading about you. You've been paying rent and you shouldn't have. Is that right?' He laughed and replied, 'Yes, and the publican doesn't want to know. I've been paying sixty pounds a week rent to this pub for the last eleven years and I didn't realise this was wrong until a policeman pulled up two weeks ago and asked me for my Street Trader's Licence. I said I didn't need one and he said I did. He went to see his superiors to settle the argument and it turned out he was right. The pub doesn't own the pavement, the local council does. So I've got to get myself a Trader's Licence otherwise I'll be in court, and I'm suing the pub because they won't give me my money back.'

One year later the brewery sold the pub. The new owners decorated the outside with hanging baskets of flowers and they didn't want Raf's stalls hiding their frontage. Raf refused to move until they offered him the use of a small shop they owned around the corner. Raf now has better premises for the same amount of rent but to date he is still in the process of suing the brewery for the back-rent he should not have paid in the first place.

1994

Steve

Steve was forty years old and lived upstairs from me with his boyfriend in a furnished flatlet. He was always very pleasant and friendly and he kept his accommodation spotlessly clean. I was aged forty-nine.

Friday mornings I worked from ten until twelve every week cleaning the house of an elderly Irish lady, Mrs Murphy, whose home was far too big for her to cope with. One Friday she showed me the spin drier she kept in her cellar and said, 'I bought this a couple of years ago when my washing machine broke down but I've only used it about six times and I don't need it anymore. Do you know anyone who would like to buy it? It's almost brand new, it's in good working order and I only want ten pounds for it so it's quite a good bargain.' I could see it was in immaculate condition but my flatlet was already overcrowded. I replied, 'It would suit me very nicely if only I had the space for it. As I haven't I'll ask the other people in the house to see if one of them would like it.' Over the weekend I spoke to the other tenants but I didn't find a buyer.

A few weeks later Steve and his boyfriend moved into one of the apartments upstairs. John, another tenant, said to me, 'Why don't you ask Steve if he wants that spin drier?' I thought for a moment and replied, 'If he does, how about I ask twenty pounds for it and you can have five pounds as it was your idea and that will leave me five pounds profit after I've given Mrs Murphy her tenner.'

Later in the day I saw Steve. I told him of Mrs Murphy's bargain, quoting the increased price, and asked him if he was interested. He replied, 'Yes please, that's exactly what I need when I'm washing out my sweaters. Thank you very much for thinking of me.'

I phoned Mrs Murphy and told her the good news and we arranged that John and I would make the collection that afternoon.

Mrs Murphy was very pleased to see us and she was so delighted with her sale she said, 'How about we go fifty-fifty on this, Sylvia? You give me five pounds and you can keep the other five pounds.' I said, 'That's very nice of you, thank you,' and gave her a five pound note.

John and I giggled as we carried the spin drier home and up the stairs to Steve, who gave me the twenty pounds we had agreed. We returned downstairs to my flatlet to split the proceeds. I gave John five pounds and kept the remaining ten pounds.

John said, 'That's what I call a very nice "sting".'

Steve was not quite so honest either. He moved out of his apartment two months later and smashed the pane of glass in one of the porch doors as he was taking his wooden bookcase out of the house. He telephoned Virginia, the agent, and told her the wind had done the damage in the night and Virginia believed him.

Cousin June

My cousin June was a wealthy widow with a desire to stretch her money as far as it would go. Her home was a beautiful bungalow near the coast. She was aged sixty-four. I was fifty.

June's only son Ivan was marrying for the second time. June decided to make the wedding photographs and wedding album a present to him and his future wife. Her next step should have been to hire a professional photographer to attend the wedding. Instead she asked her boyfriend Alan to take all the photographs.

Ivan also had money. He and his bride were expensively dressed and married in style at a Registry Office. A lavish reception was held at the local Yacht Club, of which Ivan was a member.

Alan snapped the happy couple throughout the ceremony and in the gardens of the Registry Office. He also went at great lengths to take as many photographs as possible of the bride and groom at the reception. Altogether he took over one hundred prints.

June had the films developed and to her great dismay she discovered Alan was not the good photographer she had supposed. She was embarrassed to see pictures of the happy couple outside the Registry Office minus their feet but with a good shot of a clear sky, beautiful snaps of pot plants with the newlyweds squeezed into the left of the scene, many photographs completely out of focus and quite a few with missing foreheads.

June submitted the wedding album to her son and new daughter in law with the comment, 'Not all of the photos have come out as I had hoped.' The eventual reply from her daughter-in-law was, 'Thank God we had quite a few friends taking photographs otherwise we wouldn't have had one decent snap of our wedding!'

June had a woman friend she had known for forty years and they had spent much of their lives socialising together. Unfortunately this lady was suddenly widowed for the second time. June promptly ordered a lovely wreath and had it delivered on the day of the funeral. Some time after this event had taken place June was shocked to realise she had written the name of the first husband on the card attached to the wreath.

1995

The Old Duck in Sainsburys

She was a frail old lady aged about seventy-five. I was a robust fifty.

I was in Sainsbury's supermarket waiting to pay for the food I had selected. The woman ahead of me moved up a few paces as the shopper in front of her cleared the checkout. There was no space on the conveyor belt to place my goods so I stayed in the same spot holding the store's wire basket. The old lady behind me saw the other person go forward and decided to do the same, which meant that she walked straight into me. Neither one of us altered our position so we were squashed together. As the conveyor belt cleared I placed my groceries on it and moved past the cashier to collect them. The old lady followed me and once more we were glued to each other. I didn't make any comment and quietly filled my shopping bag. I gave the cashier a note from the purse I was holding, took my change and lightly lifted my left arm to open my handbag at the same time as the old lady bent down to pick up her carrier bag with the result that my elbow poked into her right eye. She covered her eye with her hand, softly uttering, 'Oh, oh, oh.' I said, 'Sorry,' and walked away.

The four women behind the old lady were very concerned for her. 'Are you alright?' they asked. She replied weakly, 'Yes, thank you.' I turned to see them looking at me with disgust as I left the store.

It was only a very gentle and completely accidental poke in the eye but I thought to myself, 'That's what you get for being difficult.'

1995

The Black Man in Tesco

I was aged fifty.

It was a Tuesday afternoon and time for my weekly shopping trip. I made my way to Tesco's supermarket and wandered into their fruit and veg section. I decided to buy a melon but unfortunately they were hard to my touch and I didn't know whether they were ripe or not. Standing beside me was a tall, black man, aged about forty, choosing some grapes. I thought to myself, 'These melons grow in a hot country and so did he so he must know all there is to know about them.' I turned to the black man, holding the fruit in my outstretched hand, and asked him, 'Could you tell me if this is ripe please?' The black man looked at me and down at my hand. He must have realised my line of thought immediately. He didn't say a word to me. He burst into laughter as he looked from the melon to my face. Some time passed and still he was convulsed with laughter. As he was unable to speak to me I replaced the melon on the shelf and moved to Tesco's yoghurt department.

1995

The Man

He was approximately fifty-three. I was fifty.

It was a lovely summer's day and I was walking to the shops in the High Road. As I turned a corner I saw a man bending over the boot of his car, packing various bags inside. He was wearing short white shorts. As I approached him I noticed a large, dark-brown stain on the linen covering the middle of his cheeks. I decided he had a touch of diarrhoea and had broken wind without realising he was spraying his clothing. I made no comment but my mind ran away with me. I wondered if perhaps he was going to the coast for the day and when he would discover his soiled apparel.

1995

I have now completed this book and I am taking it to an agent for him to decide whether or not it's worth publishing, and I wonder if this is yet another misadventure. I will just have to wait and see.

Sylvia Smith